# The Silken
# Canopy

# The Silken Canopy

## Major Victor Dover, M.C.

*drawings by the author*

CASSELL
LONDON

CASSELL LTD.
35 Red Lion Square, London WC1R 4SG
and at Sydney, Auckland, Toronto, Johannesburg,
an affiliate of
Macmillan Publishing Co., Inc.,
New York

First published 1979

ISBN 0 304 30238 4

Printed in Great Britain by
Billing & Sons Limited, Guildford,
London and Worcester

*To those who did not survive
and for those who lost them*

# Contents

ERRATA

Page 43: *add line at foot:*
the road on the far side. It bounced once or twice and then came to

Page 77: *add line at foot:*
furniture, one piece stacked upon another—and then take a

Pages 93 and 99: transpose captions

# Illustrations

# ILLUSTRATIONS

H.R.H. Princess Marina, Duchess of Kent, inspecting the 1st
Battalion, The Queen's Own Royal West Kent Regiment
Johnny Pannell, D.C.M.
Tom Masters
Two very dead communist terrorists brought back from the jungle
Men of 'B' Company towing me out of Rawang camp in my jeep
Northern Command Cricket XI played against The Hague Cricket
Club, York, 1956 (*Yorkshire Post*)
The corner house at Westow, near York
With the then President of Rotary International, James F. Conway,
at Lake Placid in 1969

## *Maps*

*'Parachute open,*
*Parachute caught,*
*Silken flower shrivelled,*
*Blooming and taut.'*

Richard Spender, 1942

# Acknowledgements

Had I appreciated at the outset just how much would be involved in writing this book, uncomplicated as it is, I doubt if there would have been sufficient resolution to start, and if there had been, it would certainly never have been finished but for the undying patience and typing skill of Mrs Brenda Palm. I owe her and a host of good friends my gratitude for their help and encouragement.

In particular my appreciation goes to:

| | |
|---|---|
| Herr Janusz Piekalkiewicz | — for permission to reproduce the photograph of the railway bridge at Arnhem. |
| Hamish Hamilton Ltd | — for permission to quote from *The End in Africa* by Alan Moorehad. |
| Mr Gordon Horner | — for permission to reproduce one of his drawings. |
| Mr Michael Legat | — for many imparted words of wisdom. |
| Miss Mary Griffith | — for so many helpful suggestions. |

Last, but by no means least, I am for ever grateful to my sternest critic and adjuvant—my wife, Joan.

*One of the little boats of Dunkirk*

# 1

# *The End of the Beginning*

*'He who stops laughing and opens his eyes*
*Meets Death ten times before he dies.'*
Richard Spender

The whole world appeared to be burning around me and the stench of smoke and decaying flesh polluted the air. As far as one could see, in all directions, there was devastation.

My body ached and the sweat on my back was warm. The stiffness in my limbs eased as we slouched on. Only the little girl whose hands I held so tightly seemed real. I carried her high piggy-back on my shoulders and she sang 'Frère Jacques' very softly, almost inaudibly, above the clatter of wheels and dragging feet. We were making our way along the road to Dunkirk. The night was lit by the burning buildings and I felt as though I was walking through hell with an angel on my shoulders. It was better to keep moving steadily rather than take short halts; the cold night air made it difficult to start again once the legs had stiffened. There surely can be nothing more demoralizing than the anguish of a defeated army retreating and one entangled with a stream of terrified refugees.

It was 29 May, 1940. The British Expeditionary Force during the previous nine months had spent its time digging trenches to extend the Maginot Line northwards across the Belgian frontier to the English Channel. Looking back, it is almost inconceivable that both military commanders and politicians could have believed that the Third Reich might respect the neutrality of Belgium and Holland. After the rape of Czechoslovakia, and of Poland in the autumn of 1939, it became clear that the Germans intended to achieve 'Deutschland Über Alles' at whatever cost, so a hastily dug extension to the sophisticated Maginot Line was prepared. The

1

extension was not very formidable—a series of linked trenches— but they were better than nothing.

The British and French high commands decided that if the Germans invaded the Low Countries a plan, called 'Plan D', would be put into operation, a plan by which I and II Corps of the B.E.F. would advance eastwards into Belgium together with the northern group of the French armies. In retrospect it is difficult to imagine a more foolish idea; the hastily prepared defensive positions along the Belgian border would be abandoned and the Allied armies would march forward over open country to unprepared positions to meet the mightiest military machine the world had ever seen. In the event that is just what happened. The ill-trained Allied armies left their defensive positions and marched eastwards on 9 May, and in less than three weeks were in full retreat and confusion. Plan D was a disaster.

Unsupported infantry moving forward to unprepared positions in order to engage armoured opposition marches to inevitable destruction, and that comes more quickly if the enemy has air supremacy. The Germans in 1940 had air supremacy.

The rout of the British and French armies in 1940 led to the miraculous withdrawal and evacuation of the B.E.F. from Dunkirk. Hundreds of weary soldiers made their way along the roads of retreat, roads cluttered with broken-down vehicles; lorries discarded through lack of petrol; bewildered refugees with prams and little carts laden with the pathetic belongings salvaged from the wrecks of their homes; dead cattle and horses in ditches with their legs stuck in the air and their stomachs blown. 'Who the hell was responsible for all this?' was the question everybody asked.

During the day the sun was dimmed by the clouds of smoke rising to the sky and by night the heavy pall turned crimson from the reflection of smouldering buildings. The smell of burnt cordite, the moaning of the wounded and the weariness of the retreating horde provided the sickening backcloth to this holocaust.

And so it was that I found my little companion by the side of the road. She asked if anyone would take her to Dunkirk. She was perhaps seven years of age, tired and frightened. I had stopped and talked to her and was flattered that she understood my sixth-form French. Her mother and father had been killed by a bomb from an air attack and she had run away from the tragedy in her confusion. I was ashamed of the gratitude which I felt for her company. She told me that she had relatives who lived at Dunkirk—at the seaside—and if she could reach them they would look after her—and her mother and father. She did not seem to accept that the dead are gone for ever and I had no stomach to tell her. She may have been suffering from shock; her arms and stockingless legs were cold, though her hands were warm in mine. I had a sweat rag around my neck, but decided that to give her this to wear would provide her with little comfort since it was sodden and smelt like a dog's mat, and my greatcoat was too heavy.

At last we came in sight of the town. The columns of smoke rising to the sky were now thicker and blacker, reminiscent of the belching chimneys of Sheffield. We had not seen German ground troops for two days, but the Messerschmitt fighter planes kept up constant attacks upon the retreating stream of human beings regardless of sex, age or station.

I decided that Dunkirk was going to be no place for my little friend. So, with a mixture of reluctance and relief, I decided to leave her in the care of a French farmer and his wife who held a small-holding some four miles south of the town. She waved good-bye to me. 'Au revoir, au revoir,' she called, almost cheerfully. I often wonder what happened to her. Is she alive today, and if she is, I wonder if she remembers? I have forgotten her name; indeed, I am not sure that I ever knew it.

The farmer's wife, a rotund cheerful woman, accepted her little charge with eagerness. What a splendid woman she was. There was no hesitation about accepting the responsibility which I had thrust upon her. She gave me two raw eggs. I was very hungry and ate one at once, the first raw egg I had ever eaten. It was not as bad as I had imagined, previously having had only the experience of blowing through birds' eggs. The second I decided to keep to eat later and dropped it into the large outside pocket of my greatcoat. Unfortunately, it broke before I reached the beaches and, worse, it got all meshed up with a prismatic compass which I had forgotten was loose in the same pocket. I know of nothing more messy than the semi-dried contents of a broken raw egg; it also produces a very odd smell!

My small group eventually reached the beaches and was ordered to join one of the columns waiting patiently for embarkation orders. For three days and four nights we lived in fox-holes dug in the sand.

3

During the time I spent on the sandhills of Dunkirk I saw no panic or lack of discipline in spite of the fact that many groups were without officers or N.C.O.s. The men seemed to be in better order and much calmer than they had been since they had crossed the Belgian frontier some weeks before. Perhaps for the first time they knew and understood the situation. The columns were a pathetic sight, bedraggled and exhausted men with low morale but remarkable self-discipline. Foraging parties searched the deserted buildings which lined the seafront as food and water were becoming problems. Some men were too tired to move and just slept, but all used the emergency toilets in a manner which would have gratified the most fastidious sanitary inspector.

There was nothing to do except wait, hope—and reflect.

My own contribution to the fighting in Belgium had been pathetic. I was young, relatively untrained in the art of warfare, and, above all, had found myself committed to battle without clear orders and with no communication to higher formations other than by runner. In the early stages of the battle at Eekhout, near Oudenarde, my platoon was cut off by shellfire from the remainder of the company. The confusion which followed was entirely due to my inexperience, misplaced faith in verbal messages and lack of knowledge of the general situation. I had much to learn before I would be ready to command men in battle. Leading the school football team is a very different thing from leading men in war—there is no applause and there are no prizes. It may have been a half-truth that our battles were once won on the playing fields of Eton, but I doubt if experience of those playing fields would have helped anyone very much on the beaches of Dunkirk.

The few remaining men under my command had eventually linked up with the withdrawing battalion, but again, after being ordered to leave the retreating transport column without any further orders other than 'make your way to Dunkirk', like so many others we had found ourselves fighting private little battles with isolated pockets of Germans, battles for personal survival rather than part of any plan.

Now, here we all were on an exposed beach providing the enemy with excellent target practice. Nonetheless, I believe that most of the men on that beach were far less concerned about themselves than they were about the fate that awaited those at home across the Channel. Families and girlfriends who were so unprepared and completely unaware of the fearful onslaught that would soon be upon them, an onslaught which, thank God, never came, except from the air.

There was time to think whilst lying in the sun on the beaches, and time passed slowly. No doubt a number of men wondered if they would ever see home again, and no doubt some reflected on their experiences in France before the phoney war came to an end. So many of the men of the B.E.F. were young and had not tasted, prior to their first visit to France, the eager flesh passions of youth, so unlike today. Before the fighting had begun France had provided uninhibited and professional sex without embarrassment for those who felt the need or were just curious. Opportunities had been taken, and if there were feelings of conscience at the time, those feelings had now evaporated.

By the third day the columns patiently awaiting embarkation had diminished, as had the number of the varied craft lying offshore. Anxieties increased as the sound of the land battle at the perimeter became more intense and the German air attacks ominously became less frequent. The small group of soldiers decided with me that the time had come to take matters into our own hands since we seemed to be a long way from the head of the embarkation queue.

A number of window shutters (most of which were painted bright green) were collected from the derelict buildings along the seafront, together with an assortment of rubber tyres, pieces of timber, empty petrol cans, wire and rope—and a quarter of a bottle of Benedictine! A raft was constructed from the proceeds of our scavenger-hunt. It was built close to the water's edge and by midday the task was completed. After breaking the now empty bottle of Benedictine on one of the empty petrol cans and christening our craft *Floating Fanny*, we pushed it into the sea, and much to the relief of its builders it floated! We climbed on to the uneven platform as gingerly as if it were a hot tin roof, but our fears were without foundation because this noble craft remained steady and showed no sign of resenting its crew.

Rough paddles had been made, and our small party set out to cross the English Channel on a 'pea-green' raft aided by a compass encrusted with the dried contents of a raw egg!

For a time all went well, but with the shore left some four hundred yards behind something went wrong. The raft slowly started to list; two empty petrol cans broke away and as they did so the raft capsized. Those on board slid into the water and found themselves surrounded by pieces of the disintegrated home-made craft which had been constructed with such enthusiasm, if with little expertise.

I had already removed my boots and socks, but with difficulty struggled out of my greatcoat. After some twenty minutes of splashing about in the water I found myself alongside a ship of the Royal Navy and climbed the rope nets, above which eager hands lifted me aboard. However, hopes of an immediate passage back to England were quickly dispersed when some time later the ship was hit by an aerial torpedo from yet another assault by the Luftwaffe. I was flung high into the air and found myself back in the sea, but this time with a very large number of others. I am sure that many men lost their lives following that explosion, not only because no help was possible, but also because many of them just could not swim. The gurgling shouts of drowning men are fearful sounds and salt water is not kind to open wounds.

The sea was calm and fortunately I was a strong swimmer. There were boats of all shapes and sizes, seemingly everywhere, and it was not long before I reached one of these vessels—a tug from the Port of London. Several survivors had been pulled aboard this little 'sea bug'. The vision of the skipper of that Thames tug remains clear: short, thickset, unshaven, a cockney voice and a tired, anxious, but cheerful sunburned face. I felt miserable, hungry and very wet. 'Come aboard, you poor bastards,' was his greeting.

The skipper suggested that those who had been dragged from the sea should take off their clothes, wrap themselves in the blankets which he had provided, go below deck and get some sleep. It was good to hear someone at last giving orders with supreme confidence, blasphemous as they were!

Having got below, this worthy skipper produced a bottle of whisky from which were taken liberal draughts. With the sound in my ears of one of my companions saying, 'Here's to bonny Scotland—and a bloody long dram,' I fell asleep. When I awoke, appropriately the tug was in Dover harbour.

We were home, but I could not help thinking of those who were still patiently waiting on the beach. What were their chances? What would become of the neat rows of unburied dead?

Altogether over 338,000 British and French troops were evacuated from Dunkirk Harbour and the beaches around it between 28 May and 4 June. For two more weeks it was hoped that the French might by some means continue the struggle. But they were unable to stem the German tide. On 17 June the French asked for an armistice, ordering all their forces to cease fighting. On 22 June an armistice between France and Germany was signed.

For the second time in less than half a century the Germans had invaded the Low Countries for a 'short dash to the Channel ports'—and this time they had succeeded. Fortunately, the weather had been good, which had allowed the hard-pressed British Expeditionary Force, at least in part, to return home. Evacuation had offered the only hope of survival and the opportunity to fight another day.

In my Company the commander had been wounded, the second-in-command and a platoon commander had been killed, leaving only one other subaltern and myself. I had received a flesh wound in the head and some small pieces of shrapnel in my back which, when I was stripped to the buff, gave the impression that I was suffering from the black pox.

After disembarking (in the nude except for a blanket) clothing replacements were made available—how efficient and thoughtful were those at home at this time. By a roundabout route we were transported by train to Tidworth, near Aldershot. Civilians had prepared stamped postcards ready for us to write home advising anxious relatives that we had returned safely—so many had not. It was hard to continue giving negative answers to the many relatives who made inquiries about their husbands, brothers and sons. So many anxious faces and alert eyes peered into the windows of each carriage at every station where the train came to a brief halt.

The military establishments by which eventually we found ourselves surrounded were disorganized, understandably, and movement along roads near the camps went unchecked. One wondered at that time what would happen if the Führer decided to cross the Channel and invade. It was possible to wander in and out of officers' messes without being challenged. French, Belgian and British personnel were housed almost indiscriminately. Roll-calls of little groups of survivors were pathetic to see.

It was difficult to understand the warmth with which the return of the B.E.F. was welcomed. We were the remnants of a defeated

7

army, but one beaten by lack of political and military foresight, by the enemy's superior equipment and by little knowledge of modern battle techniques rather than by a lack of spirit.

By the end of the summer of 1940 the prospect of the Queen's Own Royal West Kent Regiment seeing action in the immediate future appeared to be remote, particularly as the probability of an invasion on the south coast by the Germans had receded. We will never know why the Germans did not invade these islands, neither will we ever be certain what would have been the outcome had they done so.

Attractive terms at that time were offered to volunteers for the Royal West African Frontier Force. I volunteered to serve with the Gold Coast Regiment and sailed from Avonmouth on 14 September 1940, arriving in Accra a month later. Some said that we had sailed so far west to avoid the U-boats that we might have seen the Statue of Liberty from the crow's-nest. Having spent a few weeks with the 4th Battalion we left Accra for Gambia and arrived at the sea-port capital, Bathurst, on 15 November. Many of the African troops had never been on a ship before, most were violently sick, and a little afraid. Their condition in the holds reminded me of what it must have been like in the days of the slave ships, not quite as bad, no doubt, but the mixed stench of vomiting and sweat was almost overpowering. Fortunately, the voyage was short. I remember thinking at the time that we never had African slavery in the British Isles—we just captured them and then sold them to others.

After landing the Battalion moved to a camp at Brikama some 40 miles inland in the South Kombo.

I was twenty-one years of age and my experience in France and Belgium had left deep impressions. Eleven months' service with the 4th Battalion, Gold Coast Regiment in the Gambia was just what I needed: a period of training raw, tough, enthusiastic African Troops. As I was to appreciate years later, there is no better way to learn than to be an instructor. By the time I left West Africa in October 1941, I had had many opportunities to practise battle skills under arduous conditions. I shall always be grateful to those West African soldiers with whom I trained in such an uncomfortable climate. My service in West Africa had come at a good time: the Allies were recovering from the shock of the defeat in the Low Countries and the battle of Britain in the air had been won. It was a time for licking wounds and preparing for the eventual retribution.

I also enjoyed my secondment; it taught me much: the Hausa language, the customs of many tribes, how to live in the bush, and the pleasure of eating 'groundnut chop', a very thick soup made of crushed ground-nuts (peanuts) in which is cooked large pieces of chicken or guinea fowl—the whole concoction is then laced with very, very hot red peppers.

One of the many things I find hard to forget was a barbaric system of punishment used in the Gold Coast Regiment at that time. It was called 'bulala sida', which, freely translated, means 'six for arse'. An African found guilty of an offence, which need not have been so very serious, could be given this punishment. It required him to lie on the ground, face down with his buttocks made bare. A blanket was placed over the area of his kidneys in order to prevent them incurring damage. The African Sergeant-major administered six strokes across the naked buttocks with a split bamboo cane until the nerves in that part of the anatomy quivered. I have seen an African take this punishment while blood was drawn, and at the same time toy with a blade of grass between his thumbs and forefingers, such was his pride. The 'white' British Army had given up flogging many years before; why it remained acceptable for African colonial troops is hard to excuse.

In those days the West Africans had implicit faith in 'the white man'. I received a letter from an African tribal chief, Seyfu Mafody Tomay which speaks for itself. I wish I had been able to be of some real help, but his complaint had gone unattended for too long and venereal disease was all too common in West Africa at that time. Medical services in 1940 were almost non-existent and many Africans, without proper treatment, suffered from venereal disease, ulcers and beriberi.

For the British officers and N.C.O.s (there were no white private soldiers in the Gold Coast Regiment) separation from white women for months on end was a strain, especially in the climatic conditions of the West Coast and those who were normal felt the stress. I only knew of one case of a European contracting V.D. I have always been super-conscious of this disease in view of my own initials!

The African soldier was protected because of the restrictions imposed upon him by his military duties, but this protection was

9

not absolute. However, the men from the Gold Coast were not promiscuous and separation from their families was a burden hard for them to bear, particularly as they had never experienced separation before.

The West African from the 'bush', untouched by the outside world, was proud, brave, superstitious, childlike and loyal, but it took very little time for a number of them to lose the best of these traits once they found themselves in the environment of the sea-ports and the West Coast. 'The coast boy' became a 'Christian', he sang hymns and carried a Bible under his arm—camouflage for every minor breach of the law. A little learning and the power of money quickly changed the character of the 'bushman'. Some leaders of African states today appear to suffer from an inability to segregate corruption from power newly acquired.

The District Officers—representatives of the 'Great White King'—were judges, doctors, administrators, priests and all things to the African, indeed, their responsibilities were immense. They were over-worked and because of the vast areas they had to cover their task was made doubly difficult, particularly in the rainy season. Today, one is bound to wonder if their work was wasted. In 1940 nearly every village had a picture of the King—but today I doubt if there is one single picture of H.M. The Queen hanging in a *gida*—bamboo hut—in West Africa.

Having seen West Africans dance with complete abandon to the beating of drums, no gyrating of modern youth in the western world can match the traumatic vigour of the West African dancer. After dark the women would dance in the village square until the fires were no longer bright enough to cast their shadows. I have a drum and a sword presented to me by an African chief and they are beautiful pieces of workmanship, and from time to time I cannot resist tapping the drum—the goatskin is still taut and the sound of the beat always takes me back to Brikama and the vision of black shining bodies dancing and feet with bright pink soles thumping up clouds of dust.

I bought a horse, not because I was any kind of a horseman, but because there was little with which to occupy oneself in off-duty hours. Riding, which presented an interest outside military training, seemed a good idea. I called my horse Juju, a name which proved to be more appropriate than at first I realized.

Each evening Juju (defined in the dictionary as African magic, a charm or taboo) and I trotted along the bush paths and became a source of amusement for the young children of Brikama village. Juju was aware of the fact that I was no horseman and frequently took advantage of it. I often found myself flung out of the saddle and as a consequence the greater part of my exercise was frequently taken on foot chasing a runaway horse followed by a horde of screaming black children.

A sad day arrived when I realized that Juju had been bitten by a tsetse fly; he became very sick and had to be put down. There were few horses in Gambia and even fewer people who wanted to buy an unwanted saddle—I could not afford to buy another horse and the saddle was now useless. I never did manage to sell it. I was not consoled in my loss by Jo Bo, my parrot; a remarkable bird which could speak only one sentence—'Sabra—cadunk na mutu', which means 'Shortly, I am going to die.' I think he was taught it by my orderly, Baba Mafoli, such was Baba's morbid sense of humour.

The potential German interest in Dakar had receded and the war seemed to be miles away, as indeed it was. However, there were minor excitements.

We lived in *gidas* with grass roofs. They were a kind of bedsitter, one large living-room/bedroom and a small bathroom. This had a shower unit—a kerosene tin punctured with several holes and suspended above a round canvas bath. Each evening my orderly would pour water into the kerosene tin while I stood underneath. The water drained over my head and collected in the canvas bath. When the ablutions were completed the bath was turned over in order to drain and dry it. One morning I was about to take my shower when I noticed that the tail of a snake was protruding from underneath the upturned bath. I called out for Baba Mafoli, who came at the double, and pointed to the visitor in my bathroom. Baba drew his machete, lifted up the bath and with one stroke severed the head of the intruder—a python, some fourteen feet in length. He had coiled himself up inside the upturned bath, no doubt because he found it cool. The creature took some time to accept that it was dead and the body thrashed about in my bathroom wrecking a part of the wall and most of the shelves on which I kept my shaving-brush, razor and other toilet bits and pieces. It smashed my only mirror, and mirrors in that part of the world could buy four wives! However, Baba was delighted because it meant that he could share the meat of the snake with his friends. The flesh was cut into thick steaks and the spine removed, leaving round, unpleasant-looking fillets. These were threaded on to a stick and roasted over an open fire. I never had the courage to taste this delicacy though it was much appreciated by the West African.

The skin was beautiful, but unfortunately I did not have it properly cured, and although I brought it back home with me, eventually it had to be destroyed—it smelt dreadful!

Many years after the war I met and became a friend of the late John Akar, M.B.E., then Ambassador for Sierra Leone in London. He was a very handsome man with a deep, melodious speaking voice like Paul Robeson. Little wonder that this man had a beautiful wife, the most beautiful woman I think that I have ever seen. John Akar was conscious of being unconscious about his dark skin. I remember one day, following a luncheon at the Hotel Russell in London, the waiter approached and asked if John liked his coffee 'black or white', to which the immediate reply was 'I can give you only one guess!'

John had a gift of explaining the problems of race and 'colour' more profoundly than any other man I have heard. His untimely death in the prime of life was a tragedy—how much he could have contributed to solving some current problems had he been given more time. He was a Negro with an English university education of which he was very proud. At a conference in 1969 he said:

I think that there is an essential British kindness and fair play that will never make Britain the paradise of bigots. It is hard to describe racial hatred, insults and prejudices until you are yourself the recipient of this singularly inhuman humiliation. Ask a coloured man: he knows. Ask a Jew: he knows. But the more of us who care, white and non-white alike, who want to stand up and be counted on the side of decency and human dignity, the more the world will be made a safer place for your children and my children. Perhaps then we could reverse the poignant words of the American Negro poet Langston Hughes, 'Minstrel Man':

12

THE END OF THE BEGINNING

Because my mouth is wide with laughter,
    You do not know my inner cry.
Because my feet are gay with dancing,
    You do not know I die.

I sailed for leave in England on 28 October 1941, by courtesy of
the Captain of H.M.S. *Black Swan*, the flagship of a Royal Navy
escort to a convoy heading for Liverpool. It was an uneventful
voyage except that it gave opportunities to see the Royal Navy at
work in the Atlantic and to experience its skill at protecting
convoys from German submarine packs. I also learned to overcome
seasickness; after tossing, rolling and pitching in that craft for four
weeks it was a case of surviving or giving up and dying!

I earned my keep on board by teaching some of the ratings how
to fire and maintain a Lewis gun which they had somehow
acquired. They were very quick to learn and I shared their obvious
disappointment in not having a single opportunity to fire the gun in
anger during the voyage. Come to think of it, I never learned how
they 'acquired' that gun!

While we were at sea we heard of the first aircraft carrier to be
sunk—the *Ark Royal*, in the Mediterranean. The Chief Engineer
of H.M.S. *Black Swan* had at one time served on 'the *Ark*'; he
could speak of little else—he thought it the finest ship
afloat—indeed, unsinkable. His grief when he learned that this
great aircraft carrier had been lost was plain to see—it was as
though a little of himself had died, as I think it had.


Leave in England was good, but I was restive. A return to Gambia
did not appeal to me. I had seen the West Coast and one trip was
enough. An attack of malaria led to my leave being extended,
during which I learned of the newly formed Airborne arm which
would promise immediate relief from a return to the heat of the
African bush and the sense of frustration inevitably associated with
service 'off the beaten track'. There was undeniable attraction in
the word 'parachutist' and a new branch of the Army, but those
were not the basic reasons for the wish to experience other fields.
The shadow of Belgium and Dunkirk clung—the mixture of
frustration and fear can be intoxicating.

Early in 1942 I reported to Headquarters, 1st Parachute
Brigade, stationed at Bulford, on Salisbury Plain, where I was met

13

by Captain 'Mickey' Wardle and later interviewed by the then Officer Commanding the 2nd Battalion, Lieut.-Colonel 'Goofy' Gofton-Salmond. I was accepted; and from that moment I came under the spell of 'the silken canopy'—and this is where the story really begins.

*Pegasus and Bellerophon: the insignia of British Airborne*

# 2

# *To War on Wings*

*'I have courted the Witch of War
And danced to her mad music.'*

I was sent to Hardwick Hall on the outskirts of Chesterfield—the town with a church which has a crooked spire. Here we were to learn the standard of fitness expected of parachute troops before undergoing parachute training. All movement in this establishment was at the double. How often one heard the Army physical training instructors shout, 'Double, Double, DOUBLE!' We doubled to and from all meals, to and from all parades, to and from all lectures, in fact no one ever walked—except in their sleep! The instructors were magnificent, but without mercy. Their aim was to break you if they could and they frequently succeeded.

After this initial 'prove that you are fit enough' course, we were moved to Ringway, near Manchester, for parachute training—seven jumps by day and one by night, but only after a gruelling by the instructors of the Parachute Training School who were drawn from the physical training branch of the R.A.F. These instructors were paragons of their trade, dedicated, fearless perfectionists. They had to be since one foolish mistake could cost a life and under nervous tension it was not difficult to make a simple mistake.

Of all the jumps I made, perhaps my first from a balloon was the most memorable—I think this is true of all who have made parachute descents. One sunny morning we were driven to the airfield. Before there was time to contemplate the immediate future, parachutes were handed to us—here were the bundles upon which our lives were to depend. One just hoped that the parachute in the brown bag which you held so tenderly in your arms had been packed with enthusiasm and expertise—there were ridiculous

17

stories that blankets were sometimes put into these bags by mistake! None the less, it was not easy to accept that this brown parcel tied together with string was perfectly safe. There was a lurking fear in the back of your mind that this might be the one parachute which would fail to open.

We were ushered into a large square basket linked by shrouds to a silver barrage balloon—the motor of the winch whirred and the cable paid out as the balloon lifted us upwards. The aperture at the bottom of the basket appeared large enough while we were on the ground, but once we started to make our ascent to 700 feet it seemed to get steadily smaller. As one glanced down furtively at the ground through the hole in the bottom of this creaky, flimsy basket, the cows in the field below no longer looked real. At last the winch stopped—and at that moment I thought my heart had stopped! There was only one way back to earth now—unless you were prepared to admit that you could or would not jump. I believe that it took far more courage to refuse to jump than it took to put your faith in your parachute and its packer.

Four of us were in the basket, including Ginger Ritchie, a fellow officer to whom I had taken a liking during the course, plus the sergeant instructor; the latter was probably the only occupant whose mouth was not tasting like the contents of an empty shellcase recently fired.

The sergeant offered us encouragement by saying, 'All you have to do is remember what we've tried to teach you, if you forget—well, there's an ambulance crew down there waiting to scrape you up off the ground. Just remember when you jump through that 'ole there will be nothing between 'eaven and earth except you. Your parachute will decide which place is your destination! Cheer up me lads, it'll all be over in a few jiffs.' He gave a shrieking order, 'Action stations number one! Both feet together—into the aperture. Head up. GO!' A slight upwards and outwards push, stiffen, head up, arms at the side, and you were on your way down—nothing between you and eternity except a parachute—provided that it opened.

The sergeant instructor left after the first two jumpers had gone; he leapt over the side of the basket—not through the aperture—to give Ginger and me confidence! We were left alone with the wind whistling through the shrouds of the balloon immediately above our heads. I was to go last, following Ginger. Just as he was about to make his exit he said, 'If yours doesn't open, I'll catch you on your way down.' He jumped and I followed. A drop of ninety feet, and then a gentle check; I looked up and there she was—the most beautiful parachute I had ever seen. Before I could really enjoy the relief and this new sensation of floating, the ground came up to meet me so fast that there was only time to remember 'feet and knees together!' Bump! It was all over. I felt marvellous. Nothing to it—until the next time.

I folded my 'chute, this precious bundle, and carried it to a waiting truck where a cup of tea was also waiting. There was our instructor, grinning all over his face. 'Your mothers would have been proud of you this morning, me lads, but if your girlfriends had seen the expressions on your faces as you went through that 'ole—they would 'ave been very disappointed.'

At last the course was completed. We had been worked very hard for three weeks and had sweated buckets, but there was a great feeling of satisfaction in sewing parachute wings to the right arm of your battledress jacket, no matter how bad the needlework, and donning a red beret. I am sure that feeling of satisfaction is still experienced today.

The usual 'passing-out' party was arranged and the famous song 'Jumping through the Hole' was sung—with alcoholic verve. The song was written by Flight-Lieutenant Tommy Taylor, one verse of which went something like:

> I saw the gorgeous statichute
> With camouflage design,
> I heard the Warrant Officer
> Shoot such a perfect line.
> 'This lovely bit of stuff, lads,'
> Said he, 'Upon my soul,
> Is sweeter than your sweetheart
> When you're jumping through the hole.'

It is hard to believe that parachutes were considered to be unsafe by the Royal Flying Corps in the First World War, except for those in observation balloons. When the 1st Parachute Brigade was first formed it was part of the Army Air Corps; it was not until much later that the Parachute Regiment became established in its own right.

19

I reported back to the 2nd Battalion, at Bulford Camp on Salisbury Plain. It was at once apparent that you were accepted into the fold, but it was equally clear that if you did not pull your weight, failed to keep fit, or just did not fit in, then you would be returned to your unit without delay, fuss, explanation or apology. This was the main reason why the 1st Parachute Brigade was able to take the cream from the British Army, much to the understandable chagrin of some commanding officers, especially those of infantry battalions. It was also the reason why the 1st Parachute Brigade was one of the finest fighting units in the history of the British Army. I am quite sure that it was a mistake after the war to make the Parachute Regiment a 'regular' unit instead of a unit of volunteers from all regiments.

I did not appreciate at the time (how could I?) the magnificence of the men with whom I had the privilege to serve and to call my friends. Many were to die, many were to suffer serious wounds and a number were to become legends. The comradeship and esprit de corps which I experienced while serving with these men cannot be excelled and will seldom be equalled.

It was now May 1942, and although at that time there was only one brigade of British parachute troops, two airborne operations had already taken place.

The first parachute assault had been made on 10 February 1941, with the object of destroying the Monte Vulture aqueduct in the province of Campagna, Italy. The aqueduct crossed a small stream, the Tragino, which supplied the water for the province of Apulia. The operation failed, but on the other hand caused a great deal of temporary alarm and despondency in southern Italy. An officer on that operation was Lieut. A. J. (Tony) Deane-Drummond, M.C., an officer in the Royal Corps of Signals. He was captured, as were all the others, but later escaped, as he did yet again at Arnhem.

This operation failed mainly through lack of experience in retrieving parachute troops. Rendezvous with submarines or other sea craft have to be carefully planned with great flexibility.

The second British Airborne operation took place on the night of 27/28 February 1942, and was a resounding success; it was a model of how parachute troops should be used. The attack was led by Major John Dutton Frost, a Cameronian, commanding 'C'

Company of the 2nd Battalion, 1st Parachute Brigade. The raid was made on a German radiolocation post situated close to the village of Bruneval, some twelve miles north-north-east of Le Havre. It was thought that the capture of German radar equipment and a subsequent examination of it by scientists might enable British installations to be improved, although that was doubtful, for British development in this field had always been ahead of the Germans'. However, it would certainly make it possible to discover how far the enemy had progressed, how accurate the process of detection had become and, therefore, how great a risk British bombers flying to the attack would have to accept. A price in lives was paid for the success of this attack, but nothing like the price that was paid in future parachute operations for far less success. Indeed, Prime Minister Churchill was delighted that the German defences on the northern coast of France had been 'pricked'. I doubt if equal success can be claimed, with complete confidence, of any other minor British airborne operation which took place during the war.

Honours and awards are mixed blessings since they sometimes do as much harm to morale as at other times they do good (the same can be said for honours granted in peacetime). The awards granted to those taking part in this operation were strange: those who commanded the air and sea contingents were awarded Distinguished Service Orders, while the commander of the parachutists received the Military Cross. The only casualties were suffered by the parachute troops: two killed, six wounded and six missing. General 'Boy' Browning, presumably, believed that parachute troops should be kept with a low profile.

While I was undergoing the parachute course at Ringway Lieut.-Colonel Gofton-Salmond had been taken ill and Major John Frost, M.C., was promoted to take command of the 2nd Battalion in his place. It was my good fortune to get to know John Frost very well before the war ended. He was the commander under whom I was to serve for the next two and a half years. Johnny was tall and inclined to be heavily built (not an advantage for parachuting); he had eyes that twinkled behind heavy lids, but they could, at times, flash with impatience if not anger. He grew a rather untidy moustache which he had a habit of pulling and twisting—a habit which helped to keep it rather untidy. He was a dreamer of battles

21

to be fought and to be won; there was no such thing as defeat in his dreams, dreams which became reality. Johnny Frost had a mystical magic—no need for him to write high-sounding messages to his junior commanders or to address the men whom he led with words of inspiration—here was the man himself—the very epitome of inspiration—such was the aura which surrounded him. He was sentimental, sometimes ruthless when he had to be, sometimes aloof, but always calm. I shall never know if he knew fear, but if he did, I never saw it. He chuckled rather than laughed and he chuckled easily and frequently. Johnny was a modest man, almost shy in matters which concerned himself personally. On the other hand he was frequently outspoken to officers senior to himself when he disagreed with a proposed plan of action—and he did so with authority and a conviction that was almost divine! Fate had set the course for this man who was eventually to command the men on 'the Bridge' at Arnhem, and every action which the 2nd Battalion fought during the war.

After the war I had a great desire to paint a portrait of this man who is a legend to legions and with whom I was privileged to serve, and so I did. The painting shows the bridge at Arnhem, the emblem of his greatest of many battles. From a clear September sky in 1944 the 2nd Battalion of the Parachute Regiment fought its way to the bridge and in subsequent engagements held that vital artery until the sky was obscured by a canopy of smoke. The portrait of Major-General John D. Frost, C.B., D.S.O., M.C., painted in 1978, depicts him defiant against the bridge, implacably calm, as he always was. His famous hunting-horn is missing: it was taken from him after the battle, but his shooting-stick symbolizes his/ nonchalance and his belief that a commander should never become involved with a personal weapon—his task was to command and win the battle, and not get himself into a position of personal combat. The strong light at his feet exemplifies his unshakable determination to hold ground which his battalion occupied and neither smoke nor rubble, nor the enemy, ever changed his poise or purpose.

The 1st Parachute Brigade had also been appointed commander in Brigadier Flavell, D.S.O., M.C., a very rugged officer who, after the war, stood as a Conservative candidate in a constituency in North London. I spoke from the platform at one of his meetings—something perhaps, as a regular serving officer, I should not have done. He did not gain the seat. It was probably largely my fault!

Training in the area of Bulford was not to last long. On 12 November 1942 the 1st Parachute Brigade was committed to battle. Great operations of war, for which many preparations had been made both in England and America, were launched. On that day a new Allied force, the 1st Army, made several landings on the coast of French North Africa. Not all the troops engaged in this operation went ashore from ships: some made the initial assault from the air by parachute. The object of the landings was to occupy all that part of North Africa which owed allegiance to Marshal Pétain and the Vichy régime. Most of those who dwelt in this vast fertile plain were glad to see the Allies arrive; only at the port of Oran was there major resistance, and that by the French Navy, but this was quickly overcome and it was soon in Allied hands.

The Germans were taken by surprise, but as always they were very quick to react aggressively to a dangerous threat. Rommel's Afrika Korps, recently defeated at El Alamein, was streaming westwards towards Tunis, hotly pursued by the 8th Army. The Afrika Korps now faced an enemy on both flanks and Tunis, its proposed port of evacuation, was threatened. For the first time in the war the Germans were finding themselves under great pressure and their doubts, if not contempt, for their Italian allies were growing.

It was important for the 1st Army to capture Tunis with all possible speed and General Eisenhower, the American Commander, appreciated that rather more than half-way between Algiers and Tunis was the port of Bone, which possessed a good airfield. To capture this airfield in the early stages was imperative; the 3rd Battalion of the 1st Parachute Brigade was chosen for the task. On 12 November the parachute assault was made under the command of Lieut.-Colonel R. G. Pine-Coffin—it was a race against time. The attack was unopposed and successful.

The 2nd Battalion travelled to North Africa by sea in the troopship *Cythia*. While at sea our orders were to keep all our clothes on, by day and night—not the most comfortable or hygienic way to travel in a troopship with sleeping bunks piled one upon another.

When the *Cythia* reached Algiers, late at night, she was

23

anchored half a mile offshore. We were to remain aboard until lighters could take us ashore on the following morning. At about 2 a.m. all hell broke loose. The Germans made an aerial attack on the many ships lying at anchor, ships carrying troops, stores and supplies. All lights were extinguished, but to little purpose since the flashes from the anti-aircraft guns and tracer bullets lit up the whole area. Our worthy troopship having had several near-misses was eventually hit amidships by an aerial torpedo. The ship shuddered and finally steadied, listing at about 17 degrees. In such circumstances our orders were to dress in full battle order and make our way to boat-stations on deck and be prepared to abandon ship. It was very difficult to remain upright on the sloping deck in full battle order and at the same time try and look dignified whilst calling the roll. During the rest of the night we remained on the sloping deck—no mean feat. When dawn came lighters were brought to take us ashore.

There had been no airborne casualties, but I seem to remember that three of the crew in the engine-room were killed at the time of the explosion. The *Cythia* remained in Algiers for the rest of the war as a supply ship.

How beautiful Algiers looked from the sea. On the previous night the moonlight had shone brightly on the buildings and the splendid houses which nestled in the mountains rising to the south. At first light it did not look quite so inviting, but none the less it had an air of eastern promise. I was to experience, at a later date, a few of its promises and a number of its disappointments!

On landing, our party assembled in a school playground prior to marching to Maison Cairée where the 2nd Battalion was to be billeted. Lieut. Jacky Parker, the Quartermaster, was still fussing about the stores which had been brought ashore. He was anxious that the reputation of the Thief of Baghdad should not be reinforced. Jacky Parker must have been the shortest Quartermaster in the British Army, but I doubt if he had an equal in ability to scrounge everything and anything that his 'boys' might need. He was a great fixer and once promised me a whole large tin of mixed fruit pudding, weighing about two pounds, if I could eat it at one sitting. Knowing that even if I lost the bet my stomach could not lose, I accepted; indeed, both my stomach and I won. That Quartermaster never gave me a second opportunity to prove my gourmand capacity. Long before the end of the war the 2nd

Battalion was going to owe much to this officer from the Royal Leicestershire Regiment.

While we were assembled in the enclosed school playground I remember Captain 'Dinty' Moore, of the Brigade of Guards, marching off his platoon. He gave the order, 'By the right, right wheel, quick march!' And so the troops did, but obeying the order faithfully they marched straight into a brick wall which immediately faced them. They did not stop, but piled up one behind the other thoroughly enjoying the situation. The exasperated 'Dinty' gave a further order, 'You stupid bloody soldiers—go back where you were!' Amid much laughter, in which 'Dinty' joined, the shambles reorganized itself into good order. Morale was high. 'Dinty' earned the affection of his brother-officers and of the men he commanded.

There was a story that he once lost his way whilst marching the Guard to the Bank of England. In order to arrive in time he took them to the Bank by Underground train—wearing their bearskins and with bayonets fixed! If this story is not true, then I would still like to believe that it was. 'Dinty' was a character—a real gentleman whose unconventional methods and complete disregard for danger endeared him to all who knew and served with him. Tragically, he was killed later while on reconnaissance; a carrier in which he was travelling was blown up by a mine.

At Maison Cairée the 2nd Battalion was billeted in a school; there were drawings and paintings by the children on the classroom walls. Their efforts were amusing and some of them were very good, but in these circumstances these little works of art looked so incongruous. The teachers and the children had been evacuated. I suppose that I took particular notice of these drawings because I had always been interested in art. At one time I won a scholarship to an eminent academy of art; my father was pleased and gave me five pounds—a lot of money in those days. I asked him if I should accept the scholarship, to which he replied that in his opinion there were three kinds of artist: those who lived in such areas as Chelsea and Montmartre and were rarely successful—he did not think these environments were for me; those who were illustrators and designers working in a competitive field of high pressure—he did not believe I would enjoy competitive pressures; and, finally, of course, there were the geniuses—and he did not think that I was or would be a genius. I did not take up the scholarship.

At this early stage of the invasion of Algeria it was important to take advantage of the initial success of the landings and move eastwards as rapidly as possible with the object of capturing the airfields to the south and west of Tunis. On 29 November, the 2nd Battalion was dropped near Depienne with the task of destroying the aircraft and stores on the airfield. Plans for this operation were changed more than once and at the last moment, unbelievably, it was decided that the dropping zone would have to be selected by the Battalion Commander while the airborne troops were in the air—and this he actually did!

From a tactical point of view the operation was a complete failure since it was found that neither the airfield at Depienne nor the one further north at Oudna was occupied by the Germans and no aircraft or stores were there to be destroyed. The result was that the 2nd Battalion found itself far behind enemy lines and with no communication with the assumed advancing American elements of the 1st Army. The Battalion at that time was unaware of the fact that this armoured advance had been postponed. The subsequent withdrawal of the Battalion to Medjez-el-Bab was miraculous. The Germans, as always, quickly reacted to the situation and took full advantage of it by hounding withdrawing airborne troops with armoured vehicles. The terrain was rough, the maps were inaccurate, pressure from German armoured attacks was continuous and casualties were heavy. There were two particular incidents exemplifying the spirit of the Battalion at this time.

Lieut. D. E. Crawley was temporarily blinded by a German shell during the withdrawal. He was led, hanging on to a rope, by Captain Ronnie Stark, back to Medjez-el-Bab, a distance of thirty miles. In spite of the pain in his eyes, the battles raging around him, battles he could hear but could not see, and the fact that from time to time he could not be certain whether he was with friend or with foe, at no time did he complain or falter. Doug Crawley and I were close friends and we were to fight side by side in many battles.

It was after the war that I had the pleasure of being best man at his wedding, which took place at his Regimental Depot (The Loyal Regiment) at Preston. On the eve of the wedding, after a very good dinner, we had a friendly swashbuckling duel with our swords on the staircase of the hotel at which we were staying. My wife and Doug's bride-to-be were more than a little alarmed by this dangerous horseplay, but I suspect nothing like as frightened as was the hall porter. I do not think he was so much concerned about our safety, but rather more with the damage we were doing to the balustrade of the staircase. Several wooden rails were severed and others went flying through the air. It was a wonder that the whole banister did not collapse. It proved to be an expensive evening, since we had to settle for the damage—as well as crossing the palm of the hall porter.

The other incident during the withdrawal from Oudna concerned Johnny Frost who, for the first time, rallied the men of the Battalion by sounding a hunting-horn—it was to happen on future occasions, and not always in battle! We were never quite certain whether the calls were authentic; however, in tune or not they always had the effect of rousing tired men under his command to fresh endeavours.

One of Johnny's secret ambitions was to ride the winner of the Grand National; at one time he had been M.F.H. of the Iraq Levies. His supreme confidence and ability to inspire those under his command without appearing to make a conscious effort or appear that he was under any kind of strain cannot easily be described or explained. After a battle it was very different: for a time he would retire and keep to himself. He felt the loss of his men in battle deeply, as we all did, but he took care never to refer to casualties. Before the next engagement he would be back again with the same engaging chuckle and confidence. Perhaps we should have known that destiny had marked this man to lead us at Arnhem.

It was now early December and for the rest of the North African campaign the 1st Parachute Brigade was to fight, without a break, as ordinary infantry and with the disadvantages of not having its own transport and the normal supporting infantry heavy weapons. Weeks of continuous bitter fighting followed. A. B. Austin in his book *Birth of an Army* records:

'Mixing of commandos and parachutists with ordinary infantry in hill attacks showed our weakness in man-power during the early months. Neither commandos nor parachutists have the equipment for holding a sector of the line or carrying out long attacks. Their job is to land on a coast or jump from the air with only the

27

weapons and food they can carry, fighting short, destructive battles before withdrawing or being joined by the more heavily equipped force. Their battalions are not equipped with a long column of transport vehicles to bring up the supplies which would allow them to continue the fight. We had to use both to fight our infantry battles in Tunisia with what transport they could be lent. Handicapped as they were, and not able to do the kind of work for which they had been specially trained, they held difficult gaps in the line and fought off the enemy while the later arrivals of the First Army were being trained in Tunisian fighting. The parachute brigade proved in fight after fight that they are the flower of our infantry.'

Transport was always a problem for us; we did not have our own and had to rely on the R.A.S.C. pool. I remember having to go to Battalion H.Q. just at the time when the Americans were withdrawing from the Kasserine Pass. I waited on the road waving my hands in the air hoping to get a lift in one of the American trucks. They all roared past me in a cloud of dust until at last one 6-tonner stopped. A great big Negro leaned out over the tail-board and called out to me, 'If youse want a lift—jump in quick—'cos I's retreatin', boss. Yes, sir! I's retreatin'!' I did not question his intentions, I just jumped in.

Letters from home continually asked where we were and what we were doing. Relatives read in the press of the exploits of other regiments but never a word about the parachutists. John Darcy-Dawson in his book *Tunisian Battle* wrote:

'Both officers and men had a natural desire to read about the deeds of their own regiment, and although from time to time the name of a unit would be released some units were unlucky. The parachutists, the 6th Armoured Division and the Argyll and Sutherland Highlanders were the most unfortunate, as not until almost the end of the campaign were their names released. The parachutists, who did a magnificent job throughout the campaign, were very angry at this neglect to mention them. They fought many battles, held up enemy attacks again and again by sheer willpower and courage, and were very disheartened when they read about other regiments but never themselves. So far as they were concerned they might never have been in Tunisia.

'I must confess the release of names appeared to be done very haphazardly and always with reluctance. I can understand the necessity for secrecy and agree that a particular unit should never be mentioned during the course of an action, not only because of giving information to the enemy but because it would cause distress to relatives of the men fighting the action. When prisoners have been taken and the enemy has command of the battlefield, where they can identify men killed in action, the need for keeping the name of a unit secret has passed. The parachutists, to quote one instance, were in action almost continuously. They had men killed and wounded, and prisoners were taken by the enemy. The Germans knew they were in Tunisia, and had very bitter cause to know when they came up against our paratroops.

'Likewise, the Argylls and the 6th Armoured Division were in continuous action losing prisoners to the enemy. The paratroops put up a most heroic defence against the German attempt to break through at Djebel Abiod but their name was cut out of all despatches from the front. Yet the Yorks and Lancasters, when they made their splendid bayonet charge at Sedjenane, had their name released.'

It was assumed that the outflanking assault of the 1st Army in North Africa would not only catch the Germans by surprise but would enable Tunis to fall into Allied hands without any major opposition. However, this was not to be. Rommel appreciated at once that unless he reinforced his flank to the rear his only port of withdrawal would be denied to him. In the event, the 1st Army encountered bitter fighting with highly seasoned German troops. The 1st Parachute Brigade took a major part in this campaign, not as ordinary infantry but rather as 'shock troops' to fill or to hold gaps in the line.

The R.A.S.C. vehicles and drivers upon which we had to rely changed with every move we made, and sometimes our supplies had to rely upon the vagaries of mules—courageous if stubborn and smelly little beasts. The R.A.S.C. drivers, who must have driven us over nearly every road in Tunisia and most of the mountain tracks, were a remarkable bunch of men; they had to be since they were expected to drive, read almost impossible maps, maintain their vehicles, share their rations and entertain their passengers by singing, constantly—and invariably out of tune. Without these drivers of the R.A.S.C. the 1st Army would never have reached Tunis.

It is officially recorded in *By Air to Battle,* published by H.M. Stationery Office and prepared for the Air Ministry by the Ministry of Information, that 'While it is doubtless true that to use highly trained, specialized troops to carry out continuous heavy fighting is extravagant, it is equally true that no other troops were available and that vital positions had to be captured and held. One thing is certain. The 1st Parachute Brigade earned in ninety days a reputation for gallantry, discipline and initiative unsurpassed by that of any other troops in Africa.'

This was praise indeed, but when one considers that the men lived in the open for four months, in the heat of the day and the cold of the night, with only one blanket per man, and often with nothing more than a packet of dry biscuits to last them for twenty-four hours, it is quite remarkable that they remained so fit and covered so much ground. It did not help their morale to know that workers at the London Docks were on strike and refused to load ships with supplies which were bound for North Africa. This was an episode in the war which many have forgotten, but I doubt if those soldiers who served in North Africa and went short of food after days of heavy patrolling are amongst them.

The operations in North Africa were very special to me because we were now attacking and all my training since Dunkirk was beginning to get a chance to be put to the test. There is a great gap between the dejection of a defeated soldier and the elation of one who knows that he is winning—even at a cost. The cost to the 1st Parachute Brigade in North Africa was very high, and felt long after the campaign had ended.

Of the many patrols my platoon undertook in Tunisia one remains very much in mind. It was a failure.

The Germans made a practice of moving before first light and taking up positions in observation posts during the day. They invariably used Arab huts, built on high ground. The troops called these huts 'woggeries'. After dark the Germans would abandon their look-out position and return to their lines. It was decided to visit one of these 'woggeries' which we believed the Germans used as an outpost. The patrol would make its approach during the night, set booby-traps and return to base long before first light and

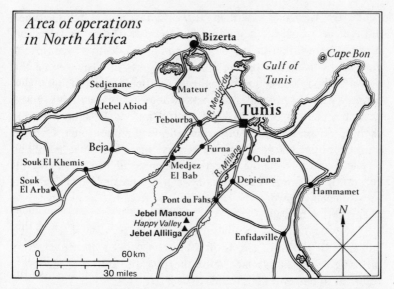

*Area of operations in North Africa*

From this map of north-east Tunisia it can be clearly seen just how far parachute troops marched behind enemy lines: Depienne to Oudna, 15 miles, Oudna to Medjez el Bab, 32 miles. The country was rough and provided very little natural cover from attacks by armoured vehicles.

before the Germans moved in. It was hoped that if the Germans did use the 'woggery' they would be caught by the booby-traps and it might be possible to gain information as to identity by a further visit to the 'woggery' on the following night. All went well on the patrol, although direction by night was difficult in the mountainous country where a prismatic compass is notoriously unreliable. Halts were frequent in order to keep control and to look back at the skyline, remembering features and so aid direction on the return journey. Night patrols are tiring because there is mental as well as physical strain—keeping direction, keeping silent and above all constantly listening. There was always the possibility of bumping into an enemy patrol—the Desert Fox, as Rommel was known, had trained his cubs well.

The 'woggery' was located and the booby-traps were set at the entrance to the hut. The traps were constructed of trip-wires at differing levels and attached to the pins of hand-grenades. We returned to our own lines well satisfied.

During the following day we listened hard for sounds which would tell us that our traps had been sprung. Nothing was heard until an hour after dusk when two very distinct explosions came from the area of the 'woggery'. It appeared that our traps had been set off. A patrol was standing by to investigate our success. This time the approach would be more difficult because there was a possibility, if not a probability, that the Germans would be waiting for us. There was also no explanation as to why the explosions went off after dusk—they should have been heard just before dawn.

Our progress to the 'woggery' was steady and sure since we had covered the same ground only the night before. No sounds were heard and all seemed peaceful enough. Then Sergeant Malloy came up to me and said, 'I'll go in and flush them out, sir.' Before I could reply he was running towards the entrance to the hut. He did not reach it. A flash and a loud explosion shattered the darkness and the silence. I felt a sharp pain in my left hand and heard Sergeant Malloy call out, 'Don't come any further, sir. The bastards have set their own traps!'

We returned to our own lines, but this time with a badly wounded N.C.O. and a platoon commander with the third finger of his left hand partly severed. The only laugh I had that night was when my batman suggested that I would now never be able to wear

32

a wedding-ring! That patrol reminded me of the maxim 'Never underestimate your enemy—especially if he is German.'

Alan Moorehead in his book *The End in Africa* wrote:

'The road near Sedjenane was so often blitzed from the air by German fighters nipping up from their fields ten minutes away, that it was closed to vehicles in the daytime. You had to park your car a mile or two back and walk on foot and under cover to the forward positions.

'This was where our parachutists fought when they were turned into ordinary infantry. No prisoners were taken in that terrible skirmishing through the rocks [not quite true]. I called on the parachutists one day, and all around the bush was heavy with the sweat and nauseating smell of bodies that were turning rotten in the sun after the rain. In their whole approach to death these young men had completely altered. They had killed so many themselves and with the bayonet. They had seen so many of their companions die. They had become so well acquainted with death they had no fear of it any longer [don't you believe it!]. The fact that that body lying over there was Bill or Jack or Jim who had eaten breakfast with them this morning was not remarkable or horrible; you either lived or you died or you got wounded, and any one of these conditions was an accepted condition [so it is in any war]. It was not that pity or grief had gone out of them, but that they were living in a well of danger and their lives were sharpened and lifted up to the point of meeting that danger directly. It was all very largely a technical matter—whether you got your machine-gun burst in first and with the right direction. These men were soaked in war. They were grown old to war in a few weeks, and all the normal uses of peace and the ambitions of peace were entirely drained out of them.' [I do not think that men will fight well unless they have faith in their cause—we had not lost faith.]

'These were the men who were flung into any part of the line that was critical. They led the forward rushes; they stopped the gaps in the retreats. They were feared by the Italians—and by the Germans—as the most terrible animals.'

The 1st Parachute Brigade fought long and hard and suffered severe casualties, and perhaps its last major encounter with the

Germans at Sedjenane was its greatest achievement. Prior to the battle a withdrawal had been made, after heavy fighting, from Sidi Mohammed el Kassin, commonly called 'Cork Wood' by the troops because of the cork trees which grew on the mountain slopes. The rain had been persistent and the red mud clung to everything. I do not think anyone really knows if it was the red berets, or the red mud at Sedjenane which stained the faces of the men and made them look like Red Indians, which earned the Brigade, and those who followed it, the name 'Röte Teufel' (Red Devil).

Following this defensive battle a message was conveyed to the 1st Parachute Brigade by General Browning in the following terms:

Subject:    *Congratulations.*
Officer Commanding:
1st Bn Parachute Regiment.
2nd Bn Parachute Regiment.
3rd Bn Parachute Regiment.
1st Parachute Sqn. R.E.
16 (Para) Fd. Amb.
Camp Cmdt. 1 Para Bde. H.Q.

'The following message has been received from General Browning and I direct that it is circulated throughout your Unit for the information of all ranks. In adding my congratulations, I would take this opportunity of expressing my thanks for the magnificent spirit displayed by all ranks during the recent battles.

To:      1 Para Bde.
From:     General Browning.

'General Alexander directs that 1 Para. Bde. be informed that reliable information from German forces in Tunisia state that 1 Para. Bde. have been given the title by the Germans of "Red Devils". General Alexander congratulates the Bde. on achieving this distinction. Such distinctions given by the enemy are seldom won in battle except by the finest fighting troops.

In the Field.                          E. W. C. Flavell. Brigadier.
8.4.43.                                           Commander.
                                        1st Parachute Brigade.'

This message was the first time the 'Red Devils' received official recognition.

The Arabs called us by another name—'the men with tails'. This distinction was no doubt due to the fact that the crutch-straps of airborne jumping smocks never seemed to remain buttoned in the front; they became unhooked and nearly always dangled as tails behind.

The Brigade was anxious to revenge the withdrawal it had made, from Sidi Mohammed el Kassin, through no fault of its own. During this withdrawal down a river-bed called 'Shit Creek'—no point in being delicate—the men had survived because the heavy artillery fire from the German guns had been ineffective, and many shells failed to explode. Our good fortune prompted Dicky Spender to exclaim:

> Thud,
> In the mud,
> Thank Gud,
> Another dud!

The outstanding recollection I have of this withdrawal is of men wading through water up to their chests with their firearms held high above their heads, thus protecting them to some degree from the shellfire. Johnny Frost on the other hand walked along the bank calling encouragement and urging us on like the cox of a university boat crew. Just how he survived the shellfire only the angels know and even they must remain mystified.

When we crawled from the water of 'the creek', everything we had, except our weapons and ammunition, was saturated. I would at that moment have given a month's pay for a hot bath and some clean clothes and dry socks—and possibly another month's pay for a very large whisky. We stank!

By 0700 hours on 27 March the 2nd Battalion had moved to an assembly area on a reverse slope west of Djebel Abiod. During the day orders were given for the night attack at Sedjenane, an attack which would finally break the German resistance and open the way to Bizerta and Tunis—Tunis the town from which Johnny Frost and the 2nd Battalion had been so near and yet so far four months earlier at Oudna.

This night attack was to be a difficult one since it necessitated

35

the negotiation of German land-mines and trip-wires which were covered by heavy artillery and machine-gun fire. For me it was to be the end of fighting in North Africa.

Doug Crawley, whose sight had now recovered, and I argued as to who should lead the Company attack. He claimed that he had more experience, while I claimed that I was the expert in dealing with trip-wires and anti-personnel mines—had I not undertaken twenty-three patrols? Micky Wardle eventually decided the issue by the spin of a coin: I won and led the attack.

I am quite sure that the School of Infantry at Warminster would not have approved this method of deciding the order of battle, but the mutual confidence of all ranks was so strong that discussions, rather than orders, sometimes took place at Company level. The senior commander's final decision was never questioned. This was not the only oddity in the 2nd Battalion: the officers initiated a record called 'The Book', in which was recorded the general opinion of what would happen to each officer in the Battalion during the next battle. It detailed whether an officer would be wounded, whether he would come through unscathed or whether he would 'buy it'. This was a morbid practice, but the book was always 'written' with much laughter, even by those whose predicted fates were unfortunate. The forecasts, however, became uncannily accurate, so much so that Johnny Frost gave strict orders that the practice would cease. After the battle of Sedjenane 'The Book' was never 'written' again. Men do strange things when under constant stress.

We waited all day patiently under cover and when darkness fell started to advance. It was rough going, uphill all the way with mines and trip-wires cunningly concealed in irregular patterns. In the dark one literally felt one's way forward, often on hands and knees. We made good progress, but the trip-wires were numerous and I did not think our good luck could last indefinitely. Then my platoon sergeant touched one of them—a touch was enough. A great yellow flame silhouetted the leading section and the explosion which accompanied it seemed to shatter the night. He fell, mortally wounded—lead pellets from an AP mine produce fearful wounds. I felt a sharp pain in my left leg, just above the kneecap. One of the metal pellets from the mine had gone through the flesh above my knee and a piece of the metal casing had buried itself in the back of my leg. I felt no pain. My thoughts were with the soldier who was lying close to my right hand; we had been together throughout the campaign—I owed him much. But there was nothing I, nor anyone else, could do for him now.

I was unable to stand on my left leg. It was numb. Doug Crawley, who was following with his platoon, came up to me and said, 'You certainly are a flaming expert with trip-wires. Bloody too, by the look of it. I'll take over now.' He never minced his words.

Before moving off Doug made sure that two other men who had been wounded were taken care of and that I was led to the white tape which we had trailed behind us in the dark. The tape was laid as a guide for the wounded to enable them to find their way back in the darkness to the Regimental Aid Post at Battalion headquarters.

To crawl away from a battlefield when wounded is a strange experience. You leave the battle behind, yet as it recedes the sounds seem to become more distinct, more recognizable, although more distant. One moment you are in the middle of the fray and confusion and the next moment you are alone in the dark.

I crawled back down the slope following the white tape. I had not made much distance when I came across a wounded soldier from 'C' Company on our right. I asked him if he knew how Dicky Spender was getting on, but he was unable to reply because of a gunshot wound he had received through his neck. Although he was no doubt in great pain he appeared to be more mobile than I and assisted me down the white tape. After what seemed an eternity we both reached the R.A.P. which was established by the railway line. Shots of morphia were pumped into our arms after which we were put to bed in a slit trench with two blankets. It was still dark and the area was under heavy shellfire.

With a constant stream of wounded arriving at the R.A.P. it was not possible to do more than dress the wounds, administer morphia and wrap the casualties up in blankets. Evacuation would be arranged at first light.

I shall not forget the courage of the soldier who shared that slit trench with me. He asked for a cigarette, by signs. We were concealed in the trench, so I lit a cigarette and passed it to him. He died before he finished smoking it. I did not realize that he was dead until I noticed that the cigarette had fallen alight on to his hand and was burning it.

While awaiting evacuation to hospital I learned that Doug Crawley had also been wounded. Micky Wardle, that great little man who had led us so well, had been killed. He had been the first airborne officer I had met at Bulford. It was not until Doug Crawley joined me in hospital that I learned that Dicky Spender had also been killed whilst attacking, single-handed, a German machine-gun post. (We had been known as Dicky 1 and Dicky 2 in the Battalion in order to avoid confusion. It took me some time to get accustomed to being called 'Dicky' without the '1' being added.)

Dicky Spender was a great loss, and for me left a gap of friendship which was never filled. 'The Book' had decided that one of us would be wounded, but it failed to forecast this tragic loss of a character who was so much more colourful than fiction.

It was during the early days at Bulford that Dicky Spender and I had met for the first time. He was the 'Laughing Cavalier' of the 2nd Battalion and much resembled him in looks. He was a keen oarsman—he loved Warwickshire and the Avon—he was a good boxer (he once taught me a lesson, but I gave him a run for his money), and a better than average rugby forward. His friends also saw in him an acutely sensitive, kind and thoughtful spirit. He brimmed over with life, coupled with a great vigour of body and mind. But few in the Battalion knew him as a poet—a cousin of Stephen Spender—since he kept his great gift very much to himself. He was once referred to as 'the Rupert Brooke of this war' by 'Peterborough' of the *Daily Telegraph*. In his short life he found a vision and a wisdom which philosophers and mystics, from their respective approaches, have struggled for a lifetime to achieve. Extracts from his poems head some of the chapters of this book.


The battle for Sedjenane was successful; the Germans were overwhelmed in spite of their determined counter-attacks. The way to Tunis was now clear for the 1st Army and the end in Africa was near.

During the campaign the First Parachute Brigade had been awarded 8 D.S.O.s, 15 M.C.s, 9 D.C.M.s, 22 M.M.s, 3 Croix de

Guerre and 1 Legion of Honour, and had suffered eighty per cent casualties in one form or another—statistics which speak for themselves.

After this final battle the Brigade was withdrawn. Re-training was soon under way prior to the next operation and reinforcements arrived from England forming what was now the 1st Airborne Division. These reinforcements were proud to join a unit which had gained for itself a reputation second to none. They arrived wearing red service stripes on the sleeves of their battledress. R.S.M. J. C. Lord, who was at that time Regimental Sergeant-Major of the 3rd Parachute Battalion, greeted the new batch of recruits in a thundering voice with, 'My name is Mr Lord. Don't call me Sergeant-Major! J. C. Lord—John, Charles—not Jesus Christ—he is God Almighty up there and I am god almighty down here! Now I think you gentlemen ought to know that if we in this Brigade were to wear service and wound stripes we'd all look like a lot of zebras! After this parade—get those stripes off!' John Charles Lord of the Brigade of Guards was perhaps the finest R.S.M. the British Army ever produced; magnificent to see on parade. Troops feared, respected and worshipped him. He finished his service as the R.S.M. at Sandhurst, having declined to take a commission on more than one occasion. He was, and remains, a great legend in the British Army.

Some thought, or rather hoped, that the Brigade, having been reinforced by the rest of the Division, would be sent back to England for operations on the 'second front' in northern Europe. They were in part correct, but this was not to be until after further operations in Sicily and Italy.

I left hospital with Doug Crawley; our wounds were not completely healed, but we were anxious to return to the Battalion in spite of the attentive care we were receiving at the hands of the female nurses. I was promoted to captain and assumed the appointment of adjutant. Doug Crawley was promoted to captain and became second-in-command, 'B' Company, then commanded by Major J. A. C. Fitch who had joined the Battalion from England. Tony Fitch was later to command the 3rd Parachute Battalion at Arnhem, and lose his life. At this time Johnny Frost recorded, 'Practically the only "military crime" committed by

members of the Brigade was that of desertion from hospital.'
Dicky Spender had already written a poem 'Tunisian Patrol'

> The Night lies with her body crookedly flung
> In agony across the sharp hills;
> By the fitful moon her nostrils are taut, quivering;
> She is tensed in cold sweat and lonely fear,
> Giving sudden birth in dark, sly, trodden places
> To her unlawful issue, blind, hideous Death.
>
> Across the pain-jerked body of the Night
> We must go, taking the new-born Death in arms,
> Holding it close, warmly to us, as our own,
> Giving it new games to play, new toys to tear apart.

*Douglas Dakota aircraft—C47*

# 3

# Sicily: Adventure on a Volcano

*'O Pegasus, winged horse of the fountain
Whose source sprang from Medusa's blood,
Carry us high over the mountain
Throw us not into the lava flood.
Neither carry us to heaven with your bridle of gold
Nor let us fall to earth as Bellerophon in the fable told.'*

In May 1943, the 2nd Battalion was moved to the Mascara area, south of Algiers, for the purpose of rehearsing for the next operation and for carrying out experiments in jumping from aircraft with equipment attached to the body, thus saving the use of containers except for transporting heavy equipment. The parachute containers were large cylindrical metal cases about seven feet long, which were a hazard since when they were released from underneath the aircraft, they dropped by parachute. They were sometimes hit parachutists during their descent, but more often failed to link up on the ground with the troops they were meant to serve.

It was not all hard work and training. We had made contact with some American nurses, and Bou Hanifia was a wonderful place for picnicking and bathing naked by moonlight—we had no bathing costumes so we had no choice. It was not necessary to be a swimmer to enjoy yourself! Anglo-American relations were never at a higher peak.

Late one evening, returning to camp from one of these trips to Bou Hanifia, we had an accident which could have proved fatal. Doug Crawley and Francis Hoyer-Millar were passengers in a jeep which I was driving. There was no moon, the lights of the jeep were poor, and I was driving very fast—too fast. Through the darkness a telegraph pole suddenly loomed up in front of me. I just could not understand why it should appear to be in the middle of the road. In fact, we had arrived at a T-junction and the pole was immediately ahead on the far side of the road. I realized this too late and drove the jeep straight ahead, just managing to miss the pole. The vehicle leapt high in the air clearing a ditch which lined a halt, fortunately the right way up. There was an ominous silence except for a hissing sound coming from under the bonnet.

Doug Crawley, who had been asleep beside me, had been shot forward, hitting his head on the windscreen. His head might have gone right through (it was as hard as a brick!) but the thump he received merely woke him up to ask in a drowsy voice, 'What the hell have we hit?'

'Nothing,' I replied, 'we just missed it!'

Francis had slumped in the rear seat and I thought for a moment that he was seriously hurt, but he was still asleep and completely oblivious of our situation. We woke him up with difficulty and all three of us did our best to assess the damage. The vehicle sagged at the front; presumably its landing had broken the front axle. The engine refused to start and even the hissing sound began to fade out. It was obvious that the jeep was beyond our repair, so we abandoned it where it had come to rest and marched four miles back to camp.

The point of relating this incident is not to emphasize the fact that we were not paragons of virtue, but to record my everlasting gratitude to our M.T. sergeant. Having told him our sad story he merely lifted his eyebrows, which I thought to be a sign of resignation, or it may have been due to the fact that he was not yet properly awake since it was two o'clock in the morning.

Before dawn he had arranged for the jeep to be recovered and by midday no one would have believed that it had ever been in an accident. The repairs which were carried out by that sergeant were nothing less than miraculous and certainly saved me from serious trouble. When he reported that all was now well he said, 'Next time you go out on a night flit, sir, you'd better take a tank and not one of my vehicles. You officers will lose this bloody war for us if you're not more careful!'

The hazards of war are numerous and many occur when not in combat. This was not the only incident in which a vehicle and I nearly came to grief.

On one of the practice jumps the wound in my leg split open. I was glad therefore, for most of the time while others were training hard, to be confined to the adjutant's desk. One day a devilishly good-looking, blond young cavalry officer marched, unannounced, into my tent. He said, without waiting for any formal introduction,

44

apart from a typical cavalry salute, 'Dicky Dover? It's good of you to have me. Brigade tell me that you will arrange for me to do a few jumps.' He was an 8th Army type wearing a neck scarf and suede 'desert boots', but I noticed that he held the rank of captain and wore the D.S.O. and the M.C. with bar. This was obviously no ordinary man with whom to play the role of the heavy adjutant. I asked him his name, to which he replied, 'Roy Farran.' He was smiling and gave the impression that his request was no more than if he had asked for a packet of dry biscuits. I tried to be courteous and sound as reasonable as my temper would allow. I disapproved of his casual attitude, particularly as I had received no warning from Brigade of his arrival and, in any case, I had more than enough to do without starting a personal training course for non-jumpers. These 8th Army types thought that they had already won the war!

I said to him, 'My dear fellow, you will need a week of preparation before you make your first jump and then, if you pass the P.T. Instructor's tests, it will take you a further week to complete your jumps—provided aircraft are available.'

This was not what Farran had in mind. 'That won't do,' he said, 'I must complete my jumps this afternoon. I'm in a hurry.' (He did not tell me at the time that he had a 'secret operation' in hand.) To cut a long story short, Roy Farran did jump that afternoon—and broke his back in the process. I visited him in hospital and soon learned that he was, indeed, no ordinary man. He was already arranging for his discharge from hospital and it was not very long before he succeeded in obtaining it. This was my first encounter with Roy Farran, but our paths were to cross again many times, in Palestine and elsewhere, and I got to like him and to respect his very special kind of courage. He was a buccaneer, and always gave me the impression that he had been born three centuries too late.

After the war Roy Farran became involved in an incident in Palestine which caused the Jewish community to look upon him with very grave disfavour, so much so that on his eventual return to England a letter-bomb was sent to him. Fate can be very cruel. That letter-bomb was opened by his brother who as a consequence was killed. Knowing Farran as I did, I believe that this tragedy probably changed his whole attitude to his purpose in life. He emigrated to a country where he started from scratch and became a most distinguished citizen.

On 7 July company commanders were briefed for the Sicily operation, known by the code name of 'Fustian'. The task of the 1st Parachute Brigade was to seize the Primosole Bridge on the Syracuse–Catania road, and to establish bridgeheads on the high ground to the south and in the plain north of the river. If this bridge could be held intact, it was estimated that the 8th Army would be saved a possible week's delay in its advance. After relief by the 8th Army, which was expected eight to twelve hours after the drop, the Brigade would co-operate in the advance to Catania and on to Messina.

The 2nd Battalion had the object of capturing and holding the high ground south of the river, consisting of three features which were given the code names of 'Johnny 1, 2 and 3'. Support was to be provided by an artillery Forward Observation Officer (F.O.O.) in wireless communication with a cruiser carrying 6-inch guns which were able to engage targets in the Battalion sector.

On 8 July, General Montgomery inspected the Battalion and complimented them on their turnout and general fitness.

After the fall of Tunis the 1st Airborne Division had become part of the 8th Army under the command of General Montgomery. As was Monty's custom, he visited the 1st Parachute Brigade, battalion by battalion. We had been carefully assembled in a hollow square formation—all neat and tidy! He drove up in his jeep into the centre of the square in a cloud of dust. The vehicle stopped; he got out and climbed on to the bonnet of the jeep and ordered the neatly assembled ranks to 'break' and come around the vehicle in order that they could hear what he had to say. It was noticed that he was wearing a red beret and not his usual black beret with the Royal Armoured Corps badge. A parachute badge adorned the red beret. I think that some of the soldiers thought that this was carrying 'morale technique' a little too far, and I recall a sergeant who was standing next to me saying, 'I bet he couldn't jump off the jeep!' Later, of course, Field-Marshal the Viscount Montgomery was to become Colonel Commandant of the Parachute Regiment. He had ways and means which did not always meet with the accord of others in high places, neither did he always, as I believe he thought, completely convince the private soldier. He was once described as the master of balance, barrage, battle and bull! None the less, there can be no doubt that he was a great 'tactical' commander. He only failed once in battle—at

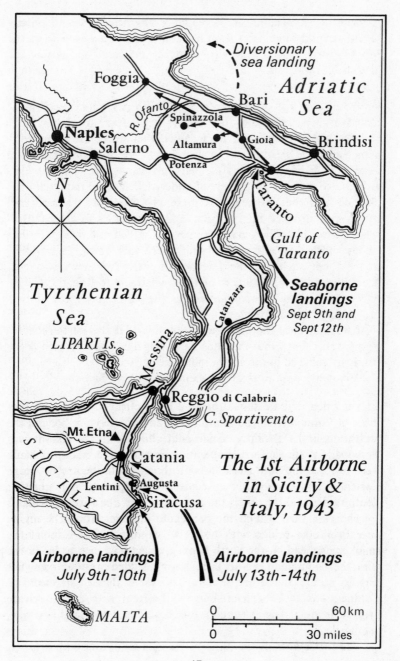

Diversionary
sea landing

Foggia

*R.Ofanto*

Bari

*Adriatic
Sea*

Spinazzola

**Naples**
Salerno

Altamura

Gioia

**Brindisi**

Potenza

Taranto

*Gulf of
Taranto*

**Seaborne
landings**
*Sept 9th and
Sept 12th*

N

*Tyrrhenian
Sea*

*LIPARI Is.*

Catanzara

Messina

Reggio di Calabria

*C. Spartivento*

Mt.Etna

*The 1st Airborne
in Sicily &
Italy, 1943*

Catania

S I C I L Y

Lentini

Augusta

Siracusa

**Airborne landings**
*July 9th-10th*

**Airborne landings**
*July 13th-14th*

*MALTA*

0              60 km

0              30 miles

47

Arnhem! R. W. Thompson, in his book *The Montgomery Legend*, says that, in his opinion, 'the vital factor of the human spirit eluded Montgomery', and that is why, perhaps, he had to act as well as play the part.

On 9 July, convoys of the United States 7th Army and the British 8th Army crossed the waters separating Africa from 'the soft underbelly of Europe' and manoeuvred themselves for an assault upon Sicily. On 10 July the invasion began. The seaborne landings were outstandingly successful, but this cannot be said of the airborne counterpart. Numbers of gliders fell short of the coast and plunged into the sea, whilst a large proportion of the airborne troops were dropped far from the landing zones. Anti-aircraft fire was opened by Allied naval forces on Allied aircraft carrying troops and as a result some aircraft were shot down. This was a tragedy, but such are the fortunes of war. This news was not heartening to those members of the 1st Parachute Brigade still in Africa waiting to be committed to the battle once the initial bridgehead had been secured.

It was not until the night of 13/14 July that the 1st Parachute Brigade was flown into the attack. A bridgehead had by then been firmly established in the southern corner of Sicily.

Montgomery states in *El Alamein to the River Sangro:*

'...I decided that we should make a great effort to break into the Plain of Catania from the Lentini area and ordered a major attack for the night 13/14 July. A parachute brigade and a commando were made available for the operation, in which the main problems were to force the bottleneck through the difficult country between Carlentini and Lentini and to secure two bridges: one north of the Lentini ridge and the other, the Primosole, over the River Simeto.

'The plan was to land the parachute brigade during the night near Primosole bridge with orders to capture it and establish a small bridgehead on the north bank. Contact was then to be made with the commando whose task, having landed west of Agnone, was to secure the other bridge. The main thrust, directed on Catania, was to be delivered by 50 Division with an armoured brigade leading. Naval support for the air and sea landings was arranged.

'The first stages of the attack were successful and both bridges

48

fell into our hands intact. The airborne operation was accomplished by a small part of the brigade, since only half the parachutists' aircraft dropped troops over the target and only a proportion of the gliders landed in the correct area.'

None the less, by 15 July the main force had linked up with the hard-pressed troops at the Primosole bridge, where they found that the demolition charges had been removed. The bridge was still intact. All approaches were secured, although the 1st Parachute Brigade had had to withdraw to a position overlooking the area.

This was the backcloth to 'Operation Fustian' in which I was to take part and yet never to see. Before the venture, we had been moved to an assembly area near Kairouan, some thirty miles to the south of Sousse. It was from this area that the 1st Brigade took off in Dakota aircraft just before sunset on the night of 13/14 July for the assault on the Primosole bridge. The planes were flown by American pilots. ('Jump in Johnny,' was their greeting, 'I'll take you for a ride.') The pilots had previously been engaged in transport duties and were not experienced in facing or evading flak. There were no other machines or crews available.

In my aircraft, No. 42, there were nineteen men, who formed a miscellaneous group. This was because it was the policy of Johnny Frost to divide Battalion H.Q. into more or less equal parts, so if one aircraft should not find the target, or was shot down, there would still be another group left to command the battalion. Each group was capable of operating and commanding independently. Johnny Frost had with him the Intelligence officer, the Signals officer (John Blunt) and the Padre (the Rev. Father B. Egan, M.C.) Subsequent events proved the wisdom of this policy, since from the operational standpoint, the personnel in aircraft No. 42 were not destined to land on, or near, the dropping zone proximate to the Primosole bridge. In this aircraft there were the second-in-command, Major Johnny Lane, his and my batman, half the medical personnel, a Brigade rear-link signaller (Corporal T. Wilson) and a number of the orderly room staff.

Morale was high and the weather was fine. The take-off was good and the Americans allowed us to smoke—that made a difference as it eased the tension of sitting and waiting. Through the open door of the aircraft I watched the sun squeeze itself below the horizon and wondered where the hell we should all be when it sank below the skyline on the morrow. For two hours the plane flew on in darkness. Night flying may be all right for the pilot who, presumably, knows where he is going, but it is no fun for a cargo of parachute troops. The world seems very far away and were it not for the twinkling lights on the wings of the other aircraft you would swear that everyone else had turned back and that your own aircraft was flying on alone.

The approach to Sicily was to be made from the east and arrival over the dropping-zone was scheduled for midnight. At about half past eleven, the crew chief informed us that we were nearing the coast and that the call 'action stations' would only be a matter of minutes. We checked our static lines, put out cigarettes, sat tight and tried hard to feel at ease. This is a time when every parachutist really feels as if the slipstream is in his stomach; if he says he does not he is either a liar or a lunatic. The message 'stand to the door' was passed down from the pilot. I was to be the first to jump and as I stood at the open door I could see the moonlight on the sea below. Suddenly the high pitch of the engines dropped as we flew low over the coastline. The change in the sound of the engines resembled the change one experiences when travelling in a car and the tyres pass from a smooth road to newly laid tarmac.

The red light came on and the line edged towards the door: only a matter of moments now! The red light went out, but was not followed by green, something outside previous experience. What had gone wrong?

The flak was light, but there was plenty of it. The aircraft began to bob up and down as if it were suspended by an elastic band. It was with difficulty that I made my way to the pilot's cabin. He told me that he had missed the dropping zone and had decided to fly round again to make another run in!

It was some minutes later, after some heavy banking by the plane, before the red light came on again; this time to be followed immediately by green. We jumped.

I was very glad to leave the aircraft. The sweetness of the cool night air cleared lungs and head. What a wonderful night it was: bright moonlight, but earth below seemed cloaked in a heavy mist. I saw to my right through the haze what appeared to be a fire. No other parachutes could be seen in the air, which may have been due to the fact that the canopies of our 'chutes were camouflaged.

I could hear no sound except the wind gently whistling through the rigging lines of my parachute and the drone of the Dakota as it flew away into the night. As the descent went on, I took a greater interest in the ground below. It looked a bit odd and it was difficult to make out any feature or landmark which should have been familiar to me from the briefing, but I could still see the bright glow which I thought to be a fire. I remember thinking, 'Thank God, they have not dropped us in the sea.' A dark mass came rapidly towards me—I crashed and remembered no more—oblivion!

When I regained consciousness, I found myself suspended in my parachute harness; it seemed as if I was still in the air. I could see nothing, not even my hand in front of my face. I thought I was blind—and then was relieved to discover that this was not so because I could see the dial of my luminous watch. Where on earth, if on earth, was I? My head ached and my back was painful as I swung gently to and fro like a child on a swing, until I felt my knees knock against brittle rock. I pushed away and on the return swing managed to hold on to what felt like a ledge. I looked up and could see the stars. It was now two o'clock in the morning. I decided that it would be best to wait for daylight before making a further move. At the moment I appeared to be safe, if stiff and very sore. I had been unconscious for over an hour.

It seemed an age before the first light of dawn appeared and then I could see that my parachute had caught on a small peak above my head. It felt secure so I used my rigging lines as scaling gear to climb the rock face. When I reached the top and looked back I found that the bottom of the ravine into which I had fallen could not be seen. I was glad I did not know this while I was clinging to the ledge during the night. My helmet was missing, I felt sick and a little giddy, my back was aching and my fingers were lacerated from clinging to the ledge.

I lay still for several minutes trying to pick up some sound of movement from other members of the 'stick'. At last I heard low voices to the right. Not sure at first whether they came from friend or foe, I made my way cautiously in the direction of the sounds. Three figures stood up and, recognizing their challenge (who the hell's that?) I joined them. Our group consisted of four, so there were yet fifteen others somewhere. The sun by now had risen and was bright through the morning mist. My batman, Corporal Wilson (Brigade Signals), and one of the orderly room staff were my three companions. All had been badly shaken by heavy

51

landings on the rocks and my batman had a nasty wound in his back.

It was clear that we had been dropped a long way from the dropping-zone. Nothing but lava rocks in all directions could be seen. We decided to remain in the area until the mist had completely cleared and meanwhile, try to find other members of the stick. So time was spent crawling about giving low whistling signals in an endeavour to locate the others. Our efforts were fruitless. When the mist lifted it was not difficult to determine where we were—on the crest of Mount Etna. This meant that we were about twenty-five miles away from the Primosole Bridge and thirty-odd miles behind the enemy lines. What had looked like a fire during my descent was the glowing crater of Mount Etna!

The lava was very brittle—like coke, and great irregular cracks, seemingly bottomless, were numerous. Only far to the south could any sign of life be observed. There was a main road built where the lava had ceased to flow. It ran approximately east to west, and on the near side there was a single track railway line parallel to the road; both disappeared from sight on entering a village to the east. A town could be seen in the distance. We studied our maps to try and find our exact position and in order to make plans to get to the Primosole Bridge area where the Battalion was presumed to be operating. Unfortunately, our maps did not include the area of Mount Etna, which complicated the situation.

There was still no sign of any other members of the stick and therefore it was deduced that some might have run into trouble during the night, because sounds of spasmodic rifle-fire had been heard a thousand yards or so away to the west. Some probably had not survived their landing—the crater was not far away! None of us had had previous experience of jumping on to a volcano.

We slowly made our way down the lava slopes. The going was difficult and made no easier by injuries which were beginning to make themselves felt. We stopped and rested frequently. Gradually we made our way southwards until the main road was clearly in view. It was then that we received our first shock.

A large party of Germans and a small number of civilians were seen marching along the road to our front. The civilians were presumably 'locals' employed to guide the Germans over the lava. The searchers halted and after a brief consultation left the road and advanced in extended order up the lava slopes towards us.

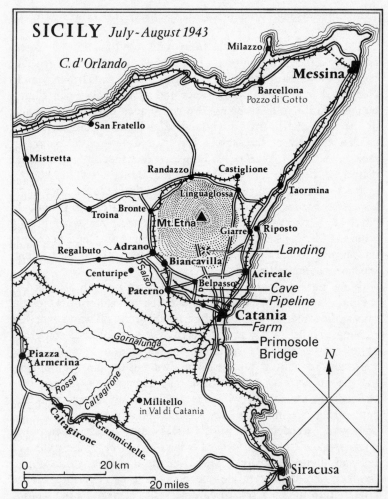

SICILY *July-August 1943*

C. d'Orlando

Milazzo

Messina

Barcellona
Pozzo di Gotto

San Fratello

Mistretta

Randazzo

Castiglione

Linguaglossa

Taormina

Bronte

Troina

Mt. Etna

Giarre

Riposto

Regalbuto

Adrano

*Landing*

Centuripe

Biancavilla

Acireale

*Cave*

Belpasso

Paterno

Salso

*Pipeline*

**Catania**

*Farm*

Gornalunga

Primosole
Bridge

*N*

Piazza
Armerina

Rossa

Caltagirone

Militello
in Val di Catania

Caltagirone

Grammichelle

Siracusa

0          20 km

0                    20 miles

This map shows the area in which Corporal Wilson and the author spent twenty-three days behind enemy lines in Sicily. It also shows that they were dropped a long way from their planned dropping zone—the Primosole bridge.

They were no doubt an anti-parachutist party with orders to search for us.

The lava stretched out from our position in all directions—rough, jagged rock formations zig-zagging without pattern—wonderful ground in which to hide. The German search-party made a pretty thorough sweep and later salvaged our 'chutes, but they failed to discover us—we had hidden ourselves down one of the deep clefts. An army could safely hide in this terrain. A civilian member of the search-party passed very close to me but took no notice; I have never been sure whether or not this was deliberate. Later events were to show that it might well have been.

It was necessary to remain hidden until darkness fell once more, because the patrol continued moving about the area throughout the day. At 7 p.m. the search was abandoned. We were greatly relieved. The constant cramped positions in hiding had been very uncomfortable and the battering we had received from our landings was now having full effect.

When darkness came we decided to carry on with all speed to the Battalion area. We clambered over the rocks down towards the railway line and main road. Before reaching the railway a pipe-line running parallel to it was discovered. We were at once concerned as to whether the pipe contained fresh water—or sewage. There were 'towers' built at regular intervals along the pipe, presumably for the purpose of maintenance. The pipe was a strange construction to see in this wilderness of lava, but a masterpiece of engineering. We made our way towards one of the 'towers'.

It was a wooden affair with a creaky door which, when pulled open, sounded to us as loud as a burglar alarm. Wilson climbed in—and almost met with immediate disaster. There was a drop of six feet immediately inside the door—a great aperture opened directly into the pipe. We discovered (after a good deal of caution and sniffing) that the pipe contained fresh drinking water, not sewage. Had Wilson fallen in he would not have survived because it would have been impossible for us to retrieve him. This pipe-line was a great find, greater than we then realized.

The ground to the south side of the road changed abruptly from lava to vineyards. We could see a small farm and hear the voices of the inhabitants. We had clambered a long way down the lava slopes and were now beginning to realize that we were all pretty badly shaken. My batman was suffering from the wound in his back and progress for him was becoming increasingly painful. It was therefore decided to remain hidden in the lava slopes and rest for a further twenty-four hours. We were all in a pretty bad way. The main battle had now been missed anyway, and our task was clearly to return to our own lines without being captured, which would be problem enough.

An excellent underground cave, one of many, was selected as a temporary hideout. It had three entrances and was well below the skyline; in fact, it was some forty feet underground. We remained in the cave for the rest of that night. The hard floor, however, was neither a resilient nor a comfortable bed for aching bodies. The following day, after much discussion, an appreciation of our situation was made:

We were some twenty-odd miles from the Primosole bridge.

Were we to make our way back to the area of operations, by the time we arrived (if we made it) the battle would be over, one way or another.

The chances of getting through the German lines without maps and over the very rough country without being discovered appeared to be remote.

The clear task was to avoid being captured and to get back to our own side of the fence. The obvious way to do this was to sit tight and wait for the battle to come to us and, at a suitable time, cross the line and rejoin our own forces. It should be only a day or two.

While awaiting the arrival of the battle, we would arrange patrols to get food and water and, at the same time, without attracting too much attention, endeavour to be a nuisance to the Germans.

This plan of action was accepted by all on the clear understanding that if anyone changed his mind he was at any time free to take an alternative course which he considered better. Although I was the most senior and strictly in command, the position was such that each man had the right to take whatever action he considered stood the most chance of success. We had all been trained to act as individuals when the situation demanded, or to act collectively—the important point was that the senior in charge was responsible for taking the decision as to whether collective or individual action was to be taken. I decided that our situation was such that no one could be sure of the best course, so individuals could make their own choice.

A sentry was posted above the cave during daylight to keep a sharp look-out for any interesting activity and, in particular, for any further enemy patrols. A reconnaissance would be made on the following evening to find a safe means of crossing the railway line and road which lay some three-quarters of a mile below us. Those not on sentry duty would sleep in order to be fresh for the patrol at night. We soon discovered that sleeping on lava is no cure for insomnia.

That day passed uneventfully. German traffic was very much in evidence on the road and many civilians also were to be seen travelling in both directions on foot and on bicycles. No sound was heard of the battle, which must surely have been taking place about the Primosole bridge. Spitfires in small formations flew overhead at intervals. Ground signals were laid out below the crest of the entrance to the cave in the forlorn hope that they might be seen from the air. Even if they had been seen nothing could have been done to help us, but it helped morale—we felt in touch, however remotely.

By nightfall, we were ready to move off on our reconnaissance, and went in two parties of two, thus reducing noise and the risk of being spotted. If things went wrong we would return to the cave independently. My partner was Corporal Wilson, the Brigade signaller. The only thing that seemed to worry him, apart from his sore arm, was the fact that he had lost his wireless set. He continually remarked on all the things he could have done if only he had had his 'bloody whisper-box'. It probably did not occur to him that had we found it the possibility of its being in working order was a hundred to one against.

The patrols were uneventful, except that they confirmed that the railway line was not in use—the rails were rusty. The road was obviously a main supply line and built some four feet above the lava. It had a wall on each side about three feet high. We replenished our water bottles from the water tower, but this was not a simple matter since the drop to the water inside the tower was such that the feet of whoever was filling the bottles had to be held firmly, otherwise there was a chance that he would fall in! If that happened there would be little hope of survival because the water in the pipe flowed very swiftly.

By the morning of 17 July we had all recovered, more or less, from the stiffness and bruises caused by our heavy landings. The forty-eight hour rations had almost been expended and our stomachs were beginning to nag. The two private soldiers thought they would not be able to hang on for very much longer without food and they therefore decided to make an attempt to get back to our own lines if no food was found that night as a result of the patrols.

Wilson and I were also feeling damned hungry, but thought that we would stand a better chance of survival by remaining where we were. For the first time we heard the sound of heavy guns in the distance. Although they sounded a long way off it seemed not unreasonable to assume that the advance of our own troops would reach our area before very long. It was hard to believe that the invasion had failed, but there was always the possibility that it had, and if so the chances of avoiding eventual capture would be remote.

The patrols that night, after a visit to the water-tower, found no food. There were many vineyards in the area, but fruit was non-existent—the vines had been stripped.

On the night of 18/19 July (five days after our landing), the two private soldiers packed their kit in preparation for their attempt to return to our own lines. The rations, such as were left, were divided, as were the grenades and ammunition, and the two set off. About twenty minutes later we heard heavy firing. We never saw them again, and later it was learned that they had not returned to the Battalion. There are some things about which one can never be sure.

Wilson and I went on a further patrol the following evening with two aims, apart from refilling our water-bottles: firstly, to try again to find food and, secondly, to cut the ground telephone-wires running parallel to the main road. Wilson as a Brigade signaller had wire clippers in his kit.

We reached the road and cut the wires. When we had climbed the low walls and crossed to the other side, Germans were heard close at hand. Three long bursts from a Schmeisser were fired and the shots went over our heads. We sank to the ground and endeavoured to control our heavy breathing. It was some time before we felt it safe to move again. After going cautiously for about twenty minutes German voices were heard once more, but this time they were much closer, so close that we could see the glow of cigarettes. In our own pockets only a few dog-ends remained; we could have done with some tobacco. We redoubled our tracks and kept to the shadows of the trees cast by the moonlight. A German sentry who was leaning against one of the trees must have heard us. We were upon him before we realized it. He turned, but before he could react he was taken from behind and a knife thrust into his back—he slithered to the ground without making a sound. A bar of chocolate and a packet of cigarettes were taken from his jacket, as well as his rifle. It was the first time I had experienced another's blood on my hands—to feel it without seeing it was unpleasant.

Of arms, we had now four 36 grenades, one .45 automatic pistol with 36 rounds, 1 Sten gun with 5 full magazines and a German rifle with one full magazine; with these it was decided that we could cause trouble to the traffic on the road.

Food became an obsession. We decided to lie up during the day, taking it in turns to keep look-out, and at night to continue to patrol for food. As a signaller Wilson was an expert, but he was comparatively unskilled in the finer arts of patrolling and moving by night. On one occasion I remember saying to him that 'I would rather take a grand piano around with me than accompany you on patrol,' to which he replied, 'If Jerry catches us, you'll need an 'arp and some prayers, not a piano!' But in spite of his lack of patrol experience there were few men in the circumstances who would have been a better companion than Wilson. Before the end of our adventure he became very skilled on patrol and more than a little cunning.

The nearest place offering any reasonable prospect of obtaining food was a German camp on the far side of the road. We therefore made this our next objective. On reaching the area, where two evenings before we had encountered the sentry, we discovered a fence of barbed wire and crawled along beside it until we came to what seemed to be an entrance to the camp. There was a sentry at the gate; he was walking up and down. While his back was turned we crawled through the gap in the wire without being seen. After creeping about for some time, we came across a cook-house—the smell, stale as it was, started our stomachs rolling. It was locked up, but outside there were three swill bins and from these we picked the daintiest morsels we could find. The Germans were very clean and orderly and the swill bins were far less obnoxious than those normally found behind British Army cook-houses. Well satisfied, a return was made to the cave, via the opening in the wire, the sentry, the road and the railway line.

On the following evening we moved off again as soon as the sun was below the horizon. It was easier to travel across the lava and avoid the ravines in twilight rather than make the whole journey in complete darkness, and it always took longer to return to the cave than to start out. We planned again to cut the wires of the communication lines which ran between the road and the railway line, but in several places this time. If this did not take too long, we would cross the road and travel in the opposite direction to that in which we had previously moved in order to see if our luck in search of food would improve. Wilson made light work of the wires. He did not just cut the wires, he burred the strands and connected different wires together, leaving no loose ends, thus making it more difficult to trace the breaks. He commented that he had probably connected German H.Q. with the local undertaker.

The job completed, we waited a chance to cross the road and continue our explorations. The small quantity of food found on the previous evening had settled well into the pit of our stomachs—we really were very hungry.

It was now that Wilson made his great discovery. I saw him with an apple clutched in both hands and feeding it to his mouth regardless of any civilized restraint. He had found an apple tree, just one, but laden with fruit, somewhat hard, but it was food. A careful note was taken of the position of the tree. We filled our pockets and jumping smocks with apples and returned in excellent spirits to the cave—like schoolboys who had successfully pinched apples from an orchard.

The following morning, we both had stomach-ache, but a few more apples eaten for breakfast seemed to ease the rumblings, and watching the Germans walking along the wire endeavouring to trace the faults helped to take our minds off our immediate problems. It took the best part of the day for them to find the faults. We laughed at the thought that we could do the same thing that evening further down the line. As darkness came we started off, and as before cut the wires, but some miles further down the road. We had become bolder and resolved to throw a 36-grenade into the first suitable open vehicle which might pass along the road.

It was not difficult to crouch behind the wall which lined the road, wait for the sound of a vehicle, bob up, throw a grenade, and then dash back into the cover of the lava.

A German half-track leading a convoy was the chosen vehicle. This was an easy target: it moved quite slowly and had dimmed lights. The grenade, luckily, went into the driver's cabin and there exploded. The vehicle crashed into the low wall on the far side of the road. There was much shouting and confusion, not only from the crashed vehicle, but also from other transport unable to pass (how loudly Germans shouted—and swore too, I believe—when they were frustrated or confused). Before long, headlamps were switched on, and the place resembled a traffic-jam in Piccadilly Circus. Germans clambered over the walls of the road in search of us; we crouched silently in the lava and listened to the possible give-away rumblings in our stomachs. The lava provided excellent cover and once ten yards from the road there was little hope of discovery. Slowly and carefully we made our way back to the cave.

When daylight came, the road was still jammed. Three Spitfires saw the chaos and finished off that which we had begun. It took all day to clear the road of the debris.

Pleased with ourselves, it was decided to rest for two days, but the real reason was that most of our time was spent—day and night—in going to a large crack in the rocks which we used as a lavatory. The apples were now causing their own explosions!

The Germans were obviously aware of the fact that airborne troops were active in the area, and therefore all movement became a great deal more risky.

Our stomachs gradually became accustomed to the diet of apples and water, but not without a good deal of discomfort in the lower regions. Our extremities felt 'red-hot'. Also, we were beginning to feel the effects of the lack of substantial food and the exertion of the patrols quickly tired us.

As the days passed our anxiety grew. No sound of the battle had been heard. We wondered if the advance of the main forces had been held up. Something must have gone wrong, and, if it had, our stay on the slopes of Etna might have to continue indefinitely. We wondered if we had made a mistake; perhaps our chances would have been better had we gone with our two companions. A daily routine, in order to pass time and take our minds off our situation, was therefore devised, as follows:

*First light*   One of us would go to the top of the cave and keep a look-out and record all that was seen. Meanwhile, the other would prepare breakfast, consisting of raw apples—mashed or unmashed.

*1200 hours*   He who had been on first watch would come down to the cave and rest; the other would take turn of duty until evening. Lunch would be prepared by the one who had rested during the morning; this would consist of raw apples—mashed or unmashed.

*1800 hours*   Discussion on what had been observed during the day and future proposals. Have the last meal of the day—apples.

*1900 hours*   Wind up watches. Mark off another day on the calendar which had been written on a sheet of a message pad. Move off on patrol.

A daily practice was made of taking off all our clothes and hanging them out to air. We were some forty feet down and therefore could not be seen, which was as well—and for more reasons than one. This routine helped to keep down the fleas which had already discovered our presence and insisted on joining us. During the day, we occupied ourselves by solving crossword puzzles self-composed on the back of sheets of a message pad.

The diet of apples was taking its toll; we were feeling low and continued to suffer a great deal of internal discomfort. As Wilson put it, 'His Adam's apple had slipped to the wrong end!'

On the night of 23/24 July, we set out with a German despatch rider as our prey. He was brought down by stretching a wire (another piece of Wilson's kit) across the road and pulling it taut as he approached. He crashed into the wall and died, I hope, instantly. It was a dangerous thing to do because the bicycle made a dreadful screeching sound as it slithered across the road and we were exposed on the open road while searching the rider. He had only a little tobacco on him—no food.

Disappointed, another visit was paid to the apple tree. On the way back to the cave we made our usual trip to the water-tower and received an unpleasant surprise. There was a German patrol moving up and down the pipe-line. We crouched, watched and wondered; our water supply was temporarily cut off. Germans apparently liked their 'brew-up' as much as anyone, and it was not long before a fire was lit and the patrol gathered together for a cup of something. This gave us a chance to get to one of the towers and water, and we took it. Thirst, I believe, will make one take risks which otherwise would not be acceptable.

The following morning, it seemed the Hun was making a determined effort to catch the parachutists who were still at large. Small groups were patrolling the area. That evening there were patrols along the road. In the circumstances it was thought best to ease activities for a day or two. Fortunately, after two nights the patrols were taken off the road and the water-towers so the inconvenience to us did not last long, which was as well, since our water bottles had been empty for twenty-four hours.

On our next nightly trip to the apple tree we ran into what was thought to be one of the night patrols, and in avoiding it we lost our way, finally finishing up south of the road close to the village.

We had come to know the shapes and formations of the lava rocks against the skyline and therefore once on the north side of the road it was a simple matter to find the cave. We always had to start on the way back from the same spot on the railway track; a handkerchief was tied each night round one of the rails to act as a marker. We crossed the road where we were able to get over the wall and make our way along the rail track until we reached the handkerchief starting-point.

The routine did not work on this occasion because, when we tried to climb over the wall, on the far side there was a drop of some twenty-five feet. We had run a long way and were both feeling done in after the detour, so we decided to walk openly up the road until it was possible to climb over the wall where the drop to the lava was only a few feet. This meant passing between two pill-boxes and, if they were manned, we would have to attempt to bluff our way through. All went well until we reached the pill-boxes. A German sentry came out and said 'Gut nacht', to which we replied '*Buona notte*', in our very best Italian. We must have been accepted as two Italians—since we were not wearing berets, belts or equipment our dress was sufficiently ragged to pass us in the darkness for Sicilian peasants. The sentry, incredibly, made no further challenge as we walked on, but our hearts were beating a lot faster than usual as we tried hard not to increase our pace or to look over our shoulders. It is an unpleasant feeling to have your back turned to an enemy when you are not sure if you have deceived him. We continued to walk slowly until out of sight of the pill-boxes and at the first opportunity we leapt over the wall, moved along the railway track to the handkerchief, and then on to the cave. How often it is that a flagrant piece of audacity is not believed and in consequence makes the seemingly impossible quite simple.

The following night I went on patrol alone. We decided to go singly and alternately in order to conserve our strength. I lost my way (which Wilson never allowed me to forget!) and found myself again in the area of the pill-boxes. I trod on a trip-wire which set off a booby-trap and a small piece of metal casing hit me in the right arm. Giving vent to a loud oath I went to earth. A German came out of one of the pill-boxes, flashed a torch about and, seeing nothing, went back—perhaps he thought it was a stray dog. I waited for about ten minutes and then returned to the cave, where Wilson dressed the slight wound in my arm and told me that I was obviously not sufficiently experienced to go on patrol alone! The conclusion that luck rather than skill was playing the larger part in our continued survival was probably justified.

The last one-man patrol to replenish our water-bottles was undertaken by Wilson. We had learnt to tie string to the water-bottles and lower them into the pipe rather than risk falling in. He left the cave at last light to make his way to the water-tower. The return trip normally took about three-quarters of an hour, but on this occasion Wilson failed to return. By six o'clock in the morning I decided that he must have given himself up, difficult as it was to accept this conclusion. I knew that I could not continue alone and began to pack the odds and ends into my small pack. I had just completed gathering my belongings together when I heard Wilson's voice. He called from the top of the cave, 'Sorry I'm late, sir, I fell down a bloody great hole and it's taken me all this time to get myself out. I've also busted a water-bottle—I think it's yours.'

My feelings were in a turmoil. How could I have ever doubted this man? How glad I was to know that I hadn't lost him—and how quickly I unpacked in order that he should not know that I had doubted his integrity. I felt ashamed, and with good reason.

On 31 July we had to accept the fact that our physical strength was rapidly declining and we were more than fed up with our enforced diet of apples—twenty-three days of them. It was decided therefore to take a chance and investigate the one small farm which had an easy approach. The farm consisted of a house which stood on a little mound; it was surrounded by a vineyard and a vegetable garden. Observations through binoculars from the cave look-out disclosed that there were three men in the house, all of whom appeared to work on the land, and three women who kept house and looked after the children. We never quite reached a decision as to just how many there were of the latter, but estimated at least four. There was a small dog, which barked loudly, and a goat. Much interest appeared to be taken by the family in a hole in the ground near to the house, and we wondered what was down the hole to necessitate such frequent visits during the day. It later transpired that this was an air-raid shelter. The family appeared to be ordinary country folk and the Germans had never been seen to visit them—a call by us seemed fairly safe.

That evening we moved in the direction of the farm and while I covered Wilson's approach he knocked on the farmhouse door; softly at first, then a final hard thump which echoed through the night. The dog barked furiously. I joined Wilson. We both felt concern at the length of time it was taking for the occupants to open the door. Eventually, with much squeaking, the door was opened—all wooden doors in the Mediterranean area seemed to creak when they were opened. A loaf and two raw eggs quickly changed hands without a word being spoken. It was all too easy—which left us with doubts about calling again. However, food was in the hand and shortly after, in the stomach. That evening two very contented parachutists returned to their cave.

We noticed on the following morning that a German vehicle stopped on the road by the farm and two German officers approached the farmhouse and entered it through the same door upon which Wilson had knocked the previous evening. Perhaps it was coincidence, but we wondered if it would be wise to visit the farm again.

It was now 1 August and the sound of 25-pounders could be heard very clearly. The Germans were making a lot of noise with demolitions. These signs were encouraging. We decided to risk paying another visit that night to the farm and obtain some more food. The Sicilian farmer was there waiting for us. He quickly ushered us into the house and shut the door. We gathered from him, by signs, since he spoke so excitedly and in a lingo which we did not understand, that the visit of the German officers had been for the purpose of obtaining wine—they had taken all that the farmer had—three bottles. He also explained, by agitated gesticulation, that another male member of the family who had seen our approach was keeping watch outside the house, so we were quite safe.

The room was approximately fifteen feet square and had only one window, on the same side as the door through which we had entered. Two of the other walls had bunk beds against them on which the children were sleeping soundly without any covers. There was a great deal of rubbish on the floor and on the table at which we were invited to sit. With much ceremony the old farmer, obviously the head of the household, introduced the other members of the family who tallied in number more or less with our previous calculations.

The room was pervaded with an overpowering smell of garlic. Our host produced a bowl of spaghetti and half a loaf of bread which we devoured like hungry dogs. The whole family showed a great eagerness to be friendly, but they were also obviously frightened. Whether this was due to the likelihood of Germans discovering them harbouring us or whether it was ourselves who frightened them, who can say? The old man continually asked when the English would arrive. He would punctuate every sentence by saying 'tedeschi', and then spit on the floor.

By the morning of 5 August, a battle could be seen some three miles to the west and by 11 o'clock it had developed on the high ground immediately to our front. Wilson and I made up our minds that it was then, or never. So we packed our kit, such as it was, and clambered over the lava towards the sound of the battle on the far side of the road. As we crossed the railway track a section of British soldiers came into view, walking stealthily in single file. We shouted to them and the response was immediate—a burst of automatic fire which splattered the lava rocks upon which we were standing. Diving for cover Wilson shouted, 'You bloody fools—we're on your side!' A long silence followed. From our sheltered position I threw my red beret up in the air. The leading scout called out, 'Are you paras?' Wilson's response was urgent. 'No, you stupid bastards—we're the babes in the wood!' This explanation apparently satisfied the leading scout who called out to us to advance with our hands on our heads.

I have never been more pleased to meet a British N.C.O. than the sergeant commanding that section of the Durham Light Infantry. He hailed us as we approached with, 'Who the hell're you?' It would have been a great moment except for the fact that we had not fully recovered from the experience of nearly being shot out of hand by the two leading scouts. They could hardly have been blamed, for we surely looked like anything but soldiers. Our boots were in tatters from scraping against the sharp and brittle lava and our unshaven faces, and general appearance, to say nothing of the smell that accompanied us, were enough to surprise anyone.

When satisfied as to our identity the sergeant took us to his company commander who provided cigarettes, the first we had had for many days. We had tried without much success to make do in the cave with cigarettes fabricated from dried compo tea leaves and the paper from the inevitable message pads.

In a very short while, we were conducted back along the road to the D.L.I.'s Headquarters. The Commanding Officer of that Battalion was very kind, but a little surprised. He was also impatient for any information which we might have of enemy dispositions. We told him that the Germans appeared to be pulling out in some disorder and mines had been laid along most of the roads. The C.O. seemed satisfied and instructed his driver to take us to the R.A.P. Here we were given the once-over, de-loused, and our minor abrasions cleaned up. Within two hours we were put aboard an ambulance destined for Floridia, a small town west of Syracuse. On the journey we passed the battle area of the 1st Parachute Brigade around the Primosole bridge, which it was good to see still intact. Along the whole route were discarded containers and parachutes; we were obviously not the only ones who had been dropped well away from the dropping-zone.

After one night in hospital, and two sleeping draughts which failed to have any effect, our journey continued to Syracuse, where a spot of trouble was encountered. The authorities had notions that we might be deserters, until a padre from the Royal Navy came to our aid and convinced the Staff of our bona fides. Padres have an authority which, on occasions, verges on the miraculous. However, Wilson concluded that our good fortune was due entirely to the fact that he 'looked like Jesus'—the beards which we had grown were as yet unshaven.

On arrival in Syracuse it was learned that the 1st Parachute Brigade had returned by sea to North Africa and, naturally, we wanted to rejoin our units with all possible speed. Everyone was concerned with going forward and had little interest in us, who wanted to go backwards. We were advised to avoid official military channels so made our way to the dock area and explained our new problem to our friend, the naval Padre. Airborne troops are always at a disadvantage when separated from their own formation—no one wants to know them since they are an administrative burden. The Padre was sympathetic and said that he would try to arrange for us to be transported by sea back to North Africa on the following day. He was true to his word.

Meanwhile, I was entertained in the naval mess which had been established in one of the Sicilian Government buildings in the town. I had on other occasions been entertained by the Navy, but this time the hospitality excelled—both in liquid and in solid refreshment. Some of the staff were Sicilian women and they had not yet gained confidence—the Germans had treated them rather roughly.

To sink into a hot bath was as near to heaven as I felt I would ever get. To feel clean after so many days—twenty-three—in the heat and dust was so good that it almost seemed worthwhile to have been filthy for so long. I began to feel civilized and as my first evening of freedom progressed so did the effect of a large quantity of Navy rum.

I slept like a log until awakened next morning to find that I had the king of hangovers and that the Padre had the passages back to Sousse highly organized. At midday on 7 August Wilson and I sailed out of Syracuse harbour. The trip was made in a Tank Landing Craft, the skipper of which also lived up to R.N. traditions of hospitality, but I was unable to take advantage—the hangover from the previous evening's festivities persisted. I did not ask Wilson how he had spent his last night in Sicily, but one look at the choppy sea and the colour of his face told me that he also had been well looked after.

The journey from Sousse to B.H.Q. was made by jeep—we scrounged a lift. And so on 9 August, just after lunch, I walked into the mess tent of the 2nd Parachute Battalion at a time when most of the officers were present. I shall not forget the warmth of the welcome extended to me by John Frost, who not unnaturally had written me off.

My only regret was that my return raised the hope that others of the Battalion who had also been posted as 'missing' might yet return. None did, and the sparkle in the eyes of John Frost gradually dimmed as the days passed with no further arrivals.

For his part in this affair, Corporal Wilson was granted an immediate award of the Military Medal. How well he had earned it.

Johnny Frost wrote to my father, unknown to me, because I had been posted as 'missing'. It was a generous letter in which he said: 'His performance is an epic and he set an example which few men of any nation could equal. He has just shown everybody here that there should be no such word as "defeat".'

This was a typical example of the generous attitude of Johnny Frost towards his officers and men. But meanwhile, he was suggesting to me that I had been absent without leave for twenty-three days and no doubt the Brigadier would want to question me about it, particularly as I had taken a Brigade corporal with me!

It was on the battlefields of North Africa and Sicily that the weapon was forged which was to be used at Arnhem. Officers and men of the 1st Parachute Brigade came to have tremendous faith in one another, and developed in themselves a confidence second to none. The Red Beret and the Pegasus sign had found their place in the scheme of things. The spirit of those days shines out from Sentries in the 'Line Book' (derived from 'shooting a line', wartime slang) which was kept in the officers' mess; typical entries were:

'I have more service watching people in the slipstream than you have in the Army.'

'Such talk makes my war wounds ache.' (Johnny Frost)

'Under shell-fire, I've lost six berets and three steel helmets.'

'It's always a fine day when I come up to the Palace.' (Johnny Frost)

'I wear my beret the way Boy Browning told me to.'

'I'm the finest type of man I know.' (Doug Crawley)

'I always go into action looking my best.'

'It's not my fault if all the girls in Grantham fall in love with me.'

'What's my name? Mine-detector Dick; that's what it is.' (The author)

'I've lived with the R.A.F. I know the right approach.'

'I'm like Montgomery. I do things only when I'm ready.'

'It is only key men like myself who know what is really going on.' (The most junior subaltern)

'Promotion will come to me the hard way, but it will come quickly.'

'I have chewed glass; chewing glass is easy.' (Johnny Frost)

'I consider it monstrous that the Brigadier should ever doubt an officer of my integrity.' (Digby Tatham-Warter)

All entries in the 'Line Book' cost two shillings on one's mess bill and the above examples were no exception.

I was given a week's leave in Algiers. Having not spent any money for some months my bank balance, for a change, was high. Johnny Frost thought it advisable that I should be accompanied on this leave by Captain Francis Hoyer-Millar, of the Black Watch; he was Intelligence Officer of the Battalion. Having been missing for over three weeks no doubt Johnny wanted to ensure that I did not lose myself again. A better companion would have been impossible to select; this fair-haired Scot who spoke French fluently also possessed a great mixture of French charm and 'Scot canny'. Like me, he enjoyed a good time, but he was also a thoughtful companion who had the good sense to leave the war behind when the opportunity occurred.

Algiers was in a very gay mood. The inhabitants believed that for them the war was over. The women looked marvellous and the lights in the city were burning brightly.

Francis and I enjoyed that leave. Perhaps the most astounding occurrence during our stay took place in a famous (infamous?) establishment called 'The Sphinx', known to every officer and other rank who visited Algiers—that doesn't mean to say all had personal experience of the establishment. 'The Sphinx' was so called because there was an effigy above the bar resembling the Sphinx in Egypt, only this one had two very prominent breasts. It was late in the evening and a number of the 'clients' had been celebrating. Without any warning two shots were fired from a pistol, with the result that a cloud of plaster dust filled the bar. When the dust cleared, both breasts of 'The Sphinx' were seen to be in sad need of repair. The bar had turned into a shambles, plaster was everywhere and the mixture of laughter, screams from the women and shouts of fury from 'Madam' foretold that it was time to leave. Who fired those two shots must remain a secret with 'The Sphinx', but I am quite certain that never again could, or did, the assailant produce two such perfect 'bull's-eyes' with successive shots from a revolver!

However, time spent in Algiers was not all spent in letting off steam. The weather was warm and most of the day was spent lying in the sun sleeping and thinking. The war had been both kind and cruel to me. To be honest, I was enjoying the excitement, the tension of being afraid and the rapturous relief of survival, but there was more to it than that. The continuous loss of men who had become close friends produced a frame of mind difficult to describe—perhaps it was pure hate. There can be no doubt that nothing stimulates more the will to fight than the loss of those who have fought with you.

I thought of Corporal Wilson, and what a remarkable fellow he was. He was married (I was single) and therefore he had much stronger legitimate motives for self-preservation than I. He was not a 'professional' soldier; he was a technician rather than a man of combat and looked like 'just an ordinary man'. I don' think I ever told him in so many words, but I think he knew that if he had not been with me in Sicily I would not have survived. He never contemplated for one moment that we would not make it back to our own lines; his morale was always high, and his keenness to wage a 'private war' was almost fanatical. He swore at me only once—and there were many times when he had good cause. The rebuke I received from him was very sharp: 'You've sat on my bloody mess tin, sir!' I did not see Corporal Wilson again until long after the war; he was then running a dry-cleaning business in Edmonton, North London. He had not changed a bit, but I doubt if many of his customers knew that he had himself sent a number of Huns to the cleaners!

If it is not a complete truth, then it is a lot more than half a truth, that wars are won by the other ranks. The finest commander and the most brilliant plan will not succeed unless the private soldier is prepared to ensure that it does.

After leave in Algiers, it was not long before further operations were contemplated. A sea-landing in Italy was in prospect. It was commented that only an assault by submarine had to be made and then the 1st Parachute Brigade would have done everything! So it seemed, then.

In September 1943, the 1st Airborne Division made its first venture as a complete Division. It landed from assault landing craft at the port of Taranto in the south of Italy. In the main, the landing was unopposed, but there were casualties in the harbour; one of the troopships hit a mine and sank and many lives were lost. It was a sad blow to the Division to lose its commander, Major-General Hopkinson, who was killed while up forward with his troops. The enemy retired too rapidly for us. We were used as infantry again, but our shortage of transport had little effect on the rate of our advance. The Germans were chased as far north as Barletta, at which time the Division went into reserve. It was the first experience of occupying enemy territory where the civilian authorities were still *in situ*. Evidence of the pernicious activities of the Fascisti abounded.

The following 'official'—and very good—advice had been published in a leaflet to our troops prior to the landings in Italy:

*The Family and Women*

Like ourselves, to the ordinary Italian, family life means everything. Families are large and united, and divorce is rare. The men are by nature jealous and, particularly in the south, keep a close check on their women. It is true that in the north the younger

71

generation of women, at least in cities, has recently acquired more liberty in their movements and activities, but as a general rule Italian women and girls are everywhere allowed less freedom in their conduct than would be thought normal in America or Great Britain. For example, it is almost unknown in the south for an unmarried girl to travel alone by train, and rare for her to engage in casual conversation with a stranger.

The main thing to remember is that a respectable unmarried girl does not walk out with a man unless they have gone through all the formalities of getting engaged. If a girl breaks this rule she runs the risk of losing her reputation and her chances of getting married. This is naturally resented by members of her family, who may also take offence at the most harmless approaches on your part.

Don't therefore think that you are going to find it easy to pick up a respectable girl in Italy without running the risk of a first-rate row, and remember that a number of Germans came to an untimely end through trying.'

For a period, a game of 'cat and mouse' was played with the Germans from the area of Bari. The 2nd Battalion was engaged in feint operations with assault landing craft to delude the enemy that landings behind their lines were projected, and this as a supporting role for a main thrust to be made in that particular part of the front. War is ever unjust; one member of the Battalion was drowned during these deception operations. The result, however, was in accordance with the object, for the Germans did think that in fact an attack was coming on that part of the line and they retained a reserve division to meet this threat, with the consequence that the real attack on another part of the front met with success, the enemy having no reserves near enough to influence the battle.

At this time I was promoted to field rank and given command of Headquarter Company. My reactions to this were contained in a letter home: 'I now command the odds and sods. Any part of the Company may be involved in a battle which I do not even see. Most of them are attached to the rifle companies; I am left with the cooks, post orderlies, and the officers' mess staff. At the same time, I am "stooge number one". I go to conferences which the C.O. does not want to be troubled with and the second-in-command has not time to attend. To any conference that is worthwhile, they both go, and I stay behind and look after Rear Headquarters. John Frost thinks the situation amusing and consoles me by saying he has had the same experience himself; a lot of help that is! What a price to pay for promotion! Meanwhile, of course, the chap to whom I have handed over the job of Adjutant, a splendid type called Duncan McLean, laughs like hell and makes damn silly jokes when he sees me. This morning he said "Sir" (pronounced accent on this title), "what you field officers really miss are your horses. I will speak to Brigade and see if they can fix you up with something!" '

It was while we were in Barletta that a great discovery was made—hundreds of bottles of Martell three-star brandy were found in a store. All the bottles were marked 'Only for use of the German Army', any other use was *verboten*. This find, therefore, was considered to be spoils of war and not loot. The bottles were distributed throughout the Division. This was an excuse to fix a celebration party and, as O.C., H.Q. Company, and President of the Mess Committee, it fell to me to make the arrangements. It was a memorable occasion and a copy of the menu is still in my possession. It is a remarkable 'document' since it contains the following signatures among those who were present:

Brigadier Gerald W. Lathbury, D.S.O., M.B.E.
   Commander, 1st Parachute Brigade. Later wounded and escaped from Arnhem.
Captain Bernard M. Egan, M.C.
   Padre (Roman Catholic) to 2nd Battalion. Escaped from Arnhem.
Lieut.-Col. John D. Frost, D.S.O., M.C.
   Officer Commanding, 2nd Battalion, later wounded whilst commanding the troops on the bridge at Arnhem. Awarded a bar to his D.S.O. at Arnhem.
Major J. (Tony) A. C. Fitch
   Second-in-Command 2nd Battalion. Later commanded 3rd Battalion and killed at Arnhem.
Major Digby Tatham-Warter
   Commander 'A' Company, 2nd Battalion, of umbrella fame. Escaped from Arnhem and awarded the D.S.O.

Major Douglas D. E. Crawley, M.C.
Commander 'B' Company, wounded at Arnhem, and awarded a bar to his M.C.

Captain Francis Hoyer-Millar
Intelligence Officer, later Second-in-Command 'B' Company at Arnhem, and awarded the M.C.

Captain Jimmy W. Logan, D.S.O.
Medical officer, 2nd Battalion—awarded Dutch Bronze Lion at Arnhem.

Lieut. ('Loopy') R. H. Levien
Platoon commander 'B' Company—and at Arnhem.

Captain J. (Tim) Timothy, M.C.
Bruneval, and dropped behind the enemy lines in Italy to assist P.O.W.s to escape, also at Arnhem.

Captain ('Bucky') C. D. Boiteux-Buchanan, M.C.
Captured in North Africa, escaped. Battalion Intelligence Officer. Killed at Arnhem.

Captain (Dicky) R. E. Morton
Second-in-Command 'C' Company at Arnhem.

Lieut. (Jack) A. J. McDermott
'A' Company, killed at Arnhem.

Captain (Tony) A. M. Frank, M.C.
Second-in-Command 'A' Company, awarded American Silver Star at Arnhem and escaped.

Lieut. (Peter) P. H. Barry
Platoon Commander 'C' Company, wounded at Arnhem.

Lieut. (Jack) J. H. Greyburn
Platoon Commander, 'A' Company, awarded posthumous Victoria Cross at Arnhem.

Captain (Duncan) D. W. McLean
Adjutant, and at Arnhem.

Lieut. (Johnny) de la P. Monsell
Support Company, and at Arnhem.

Major Victor (Dicky) Dover, M.C.
Adjutant, later Commander H.Q. Company and Commander 'C' Company at Arnhem.

Lieut. (Peter) P. H. Cane,
Platoon Commander, 'B' Company. Killed at Arnhem.

Lieut. (Bobby) J. G. Blunt
Signals officer—wounded at Arnhem.

The Italians were demoralized, their soldiers had been treated as inferiors by the Germans, Mussolini had capitulated and left his post, and now they were expected to change their allegiance overnight. Little wonder they were confused and frightened. At first, the civilians kept off the streets in the towns and all shops were closed. However, when they discovered that the Allies had not come to pillage and rape, they gradually opened the windows of their houses and took down the shutters of their shops. It was not long before the British soldier discovered that the Italians do make the best ice cream in the world—trade became brisk. I believe it was Italian ice cream which played a large part in breaking the ice!

The 1st Airborne Brigade was not to be held long in Italy. It was needed elsewhere and was to go 'home' first. The move back to England was 'top secret'. Accordingly, the Brigade was to be relieved by another formation of paratroops. These marched into the barracks one evening without wearing parachute flashes or red berets. The following morning, the 1st Brigade moved out, also lacking the distinguishing airborne markings and wearing khaki 'fore-and-aft' caps—the most stupid piece of headgear ever designed, and well deserving its other name. Meanwhile, the replacements had put up their airborne flashes and wore their red berets in the hope that no outsider would be wise to the switch.

On the voyage home, bets had been exchanged as to whether there would be an official welcome on arrival; those who gambled that a band would be in attendance, strangely enough, collected.

*Tiger tank—11 SS Panzer Corps, Arnhem*

# 4

# *Arnhem: The Lost Company*

*'The plain fact is that the First Airborne Division had been
parachuted out upon a hopeless and impossible limb in
accordance with a vain and irresponsibly optimistic plan,
inadequately thought out.'*
Captain R. W. Thompson, Second Army War Correspondent

Then began what is most irksome to troops who have known almost
continuous action: a period of re-training and waiting, with
uncertainty as their constant handmaiden. On reflection I am glad
that I did not know that my last action in the war would be a
defeat as was my first, but with one difference—this time I did not
escape.

The 2nd Battalion was based at Stoke Rochford, just south of
Grantham, and for nearly four months following D-Day it trained,
received numerous briefings for operations which never took place,
and listened to the news from the 'second front'. The 6th Airborne
Division had been committed on D-Day and the 1st Division was
held back in reserve. How frustrating—and nerve-racking—was
this period of waiting to be called to battle.

Grantham is a town which will remain a very special town to
surviving members of the 2nd Battalion, The Parachute Regiment.
The Angel and The George hotels were the hosts to many parties,
but perhaps The Blue Horse—at Great Ponton—between Stoke
Rochford and Grantham—was the favourite rendezvous (did not
Bellerophon ride on a blue horse?) I visited the Blue Horse some
twenty-eight years later; there was still a red beret behind the bar
and a framed photograph of the officers of the 2nd Battalion
hanging on the wall. When I saw them a cloud of nostalgia crept
over me. I seemed to hear the sound of voices, laughter, joking and
horseplay of 1944. No doubt there are a number of residents in
Grantham who will not forget the robust parachute troops who
'invaded' their town prior to the battle of Arnhem.

On 25 February 1944 I celebrated my twenty-fifth birthday at
the Blue Horse with a number of officers from the 2nd Battalion.
It was the custom at a late hour at these parties to pile pieces of

running jump over them. As the stack became higher so it became more difficult to clear the obstacles and certainly more dangerous. I found myself the final competitor with Digby Tatham-Warter. He was over six feet tall whereas I was a mere 5 ft 8½ inches. Digby cleared the obstacles with some ease, while I just caught the solid oak stool at the top of the pile with my toe. I fell on my back on the far side and watched the stool wobble. Before I could move it fell on to my mouth as I lay on the floor. What a mess! The party ended. Jimmy Logan put three stitches in my upper lip—and I took nourishment for the next two weeks through a straw!

Very soon after settling in at Stoke Rochford I was given command of 'C' Company—of Bruneval fame. The Company was very dear to the heart of Johnny Frost for obvious reasons, and in particular because 95 per cent of the N.C.O.s and men came from Scottish regiments—a Sassenach was to command them, and what a great privilege this was to be for him.

It was not long after assuming command of this magnificent Company of veterans that I found myself in what could have been serious trouble. Doug Crawley, who was now commanding 'B' Company, accompanied me to a social function. During the evening we met two very charming Wren officers, and at the end of the party we offered to take them home—their home. At the time they were on leave and were staying with parents who lived at a village close by.

When we arrived at our destination, our driver was asked to return at 10.30 p.m. to take us back to camp. At 11 p.m. he had not arrived and we became a little anxious. However, he drove up to the house at about 11.30 p.m. and explained that he was late because a policeman had stopped him in the village after he had left us and asked why he had been carrying civilian passengers in a military vehicle (the two young ladies were in civilian clothes). The driver told the policeman that all his passengers were officers, whereupon the constable asked for their names. The driver told him that he did not know, which was not quite true. The policeman took his particulars and advised him that the matter would be reported.

On hearing this story Doug Crawley and I became furious, since it appeared to us that a private soldier was to be reported for an alleged offence for which he was not responsible. We ordered our driver to take us to the local police station—and this was where the trouble started!

The sergeant on duty to whom we explained the facts advised that there was absolutely nothing he could do about the report on our driver, although I told him I was the officer in charge of the vehicle. If an irregularity had been committed it was my responsibility. I demanded (and that is an accurate description) to see the senior officer of the station, who eventually appeared, after a lot of argument, in his night-shirt. Some more heated exchanges took place, after which Doug Crawley and I left the police station in high dudgeon having failed in our purpose. By the following morning we had cooled off and I reported to John Frost, as dispassionately as I could, the events of the previous evening. He just laughed and said we would have to wait and see what action, if any, the civil police would take.

Time passed and we heard nothing further and I began to assume that the matter had been forgotten. However, one morning, while on the range with my Company, I was summoned to Brigade Headquarters. The Brigade Major received me in most friendly terms, but gave a warning that the Brigadier was not in a happy mood. I was duly marched in front of the Brigade Commander, Brigadier G. W. Lathbury, who came straight to the point: 'Dicky, you have made an ass of yourself! What's all this nonsense I have been reading in a report from the police about irregular use of a WD vehicle?'

I did my best to explain, but knew that I was pleading a lost cause. The Brigadier listened patiently and then, looking straight at me, said, 'I expect far better things of you than this. You can't go about telling a police officer that he has no authority when attired only in his night-shirt! I have no power to punish you, but will you accept my punishment, or will you see the Divisional Commander?'

I replied, almost too quickly, 'I'll take your punishment, sir.' The punishment came as a shock—'Fourteen days confined to barracks.'

For the next fourteen days I had to remain (as a field officer!) within my own Company lines, unless out on official training. My brother-officers thoroughly enjoyed the situation and before they left camp to besport themselves in the town they would say, 'It's jolly good of you, sir, to do duty officer again for us tonight.'

I suppose my 'confinement' had lasted for ten days or so when I was paid a surprise visit by Brigadier Lathbury. He strode into our small deserted Company mess one evening and said, 'Hallo, Dicky, I thought I would just call in and share a whisky with you—seeing you are by yourself.' What in fact I knew he was doing was checking up on me to ensure that I was complying with his punishment. He had his drink and joined me in casual conversation for about ten minutes, then left without any reference as to whether or not I was enjoying the punishment which he had no authority to give, and which I had volunteered to accept. I am certain he enjoyed that visit.

And then, at last, came Arnhem. The 1st Brigade was originally briefed a week before the actual assault, but as usual the briefing was cancelled and a number of troops went on leave. The following weekend all leave was stopped—Arnhem was on again. The general feeling about it, like all other previously cancelled briefings, was that Arnhem would not take place. If they had now decided to use the whole Division instead of the 1st Brigade, as originally intended, there was something very fishy about it.

How wrong we were! On Sunday morning, 17 September 1944, the 1st British Airborne Division took to the sky. It was to be a day of decision and magnificent disaster.

So much has been written and filmed about the battle of Arnhem that one could readily accept that there is nothing more to be told. However, there was one decision made by Lieut.-Colonel John Frost which has not previously been recounted and which may have had a decisive influence upon events. At times John Frost seemed to have the gift of third as well as second sight. He decided when giving his orders before the battle the 'C' Company would have the task of capturing the railway bridge which crossed the river. Should the Germans blow the bridge before it could be crossed by 'C' Company then the Company would enter the town of Arnhem by way of Utrecht Street and capture the German Headquarters. The remainder of the Battalion would approach the road bridge by way of the towpath north of the river bank. Just how important this alternative plan would prove to be was not appreciated at the time, but it will emerge as the part played by 'C' Company in the battle is related. Had John Frost not foreseen the possibility of the railway bridge not falling into our hands intact the main body of the 2nd battalion might never have reached the road bridge.

Those who know of this battle will recall that Montgomery planned to capture the three bridges which crossed the Maas, the Waal and the Neder Rijn, and thus open a corridor into the heart of Germany. Through this corridor the Allied Forces would push into the Ruhr and, it was hoped, knock Germany out of the war before Christmas 1944. The first two bridges were to be secured by American paratroops, but the third bridge which crossed the Neder Rijn at Arnhem was to be held by British airborne troops and the Polish Parachute Brigade.

The 1st British Airborne Division was assigned the task of capturing the Arnhem road bridge. In the event only the 2nd Battalion of the 1st Parachute Brigade, plus a few others, reached the bridge. They captured it, and held it for far longer than their orders demanded. At last they were overwhelmed. 'C' Company of the 2nd Battalion failed to reach the bridge and that which follows explains why. It also explains, possibly, why the remainder of the 2nd Battalion did reach the bridge. The rest of the 1st Airborne Division, with few exceptions, only managed to reach the fringe of the town.

On that fatal Sunday in September 1944, we rose soon after dawn. The briefing had been completed on the previous evening and all we had to do was to give a final check to our kit, get into the troop-carrying vehicles and move to Saltby airfield. The aircraft in which we were to fly—the same old two-engined bulbous Dakotas—were parked around the runway like horses in the paddock waiting to move to the start line.

The take-off was due at 10.00 hours, but the long period of time before we emplaned was not wasted. There was much to do: 'chutes had to be collected and fitted—how many times did we wonder if the 'chute, which we had drawn from the hundreds which were stacked, was one which had been packed in a hurry? The containers which held our precious heavy equipment had to be fixed to the belly of the aircraft; and then there was the final cup of tea—army tea on which, it is said, lead will float! I could never drink army tea, it always upset my stomach—it also had the same effect as apples on my rear end.

The wait before the take-off was an anxious time, a time to

think about what lay ahead. Would we find the correct dropping-zone, or would we be spattered all over the dykes of Holland as we had been spattered all over Sicily? Would we be attacked in the air? This was always a disturbing thought since Dakotas had neither armour nor armament.

A good deal of care had been taken to see that the men received a fat-free breakfast and it did not help to find a rotund, well-meaning NAAFI woman handing out bacon sandwiches just as we were about to emplane. However, the troops were in great form and it would have taken more than a few rashers of bacon to upset them.

At last the engines of the aircraft throbbed and the first strings of the flight began to move out of their parking areas on to the runway. The co-pilot came aft and told us that we were about to take off—as if we did not know! I was never sick on these trips, but I got so near it so often at this stage that I might just as well have been. I believe that every man feels a sinking in his stomach at some time, and my worst moments were always those just before take-off. But once airborne there was no going back—one was committed and the 'sickness' feeling evaporated.

The engines roared and we began to move forward faster, and faster, until we were swept up into the air.

There is not much room in an aircraft when loaded with airborne troops plus their equipment, and it is difficult even to turn and look out of the small windows in the fuselage. If you happen to be near the door, which is left open, then you get fresh air and a good view; if not, you get no view, only the smell of sweating bodies.

Once airborne there is nothing to do except to wait, and to think. My thoughts turned to that part of the operation which the 1st Parachute Brigade was to play. The Brigade was to capture the road bridge at Arnhem and establish a defensive perimeter around it to the north and to the south. This bridgehead was to be held until the Guards Armoured Division of 30 Corps, 21st Army Group, linked up by land and then for them to break out of the bridgehead which the Brigade would have formed. General Browning had said that he thought it was a bridge too far! The bridge was certainly a long way inside enemy-occupied territory and about seven miles from the dropping-zone.

The 1st Battalion, commanded by Lieut.-Colonel David Dobie,

After an investiture held by H.M. King George VI in 1944. The famous 'yellow lanyard', worn round the left shoulder, was made from old grey or white parachute lines dyed in a solution of the brilliant yellow Mecaprine tablets used as a substitute for quinine.

Richard W. O. Spender, the 'Laughing Cavalier', who wrote of the little men who die for the salvation of the great truths. He lost his life charging a German machine-gun post single-handed. Dicky saw himself in a modest light and was quite unaware that wherever he moved he brought gaiety, poetry and laughter to those in his company.

How not to make an exit—legs wide apart and the danger of going into a spin.
The jumper whose parachute is about to develop has made a good exit, but he is
uncomfortably close to one of the heavy containers in which arms and supplies were
dropped. These jumps were being made through a hole in the fuselage before door
exits were introduced.

To Mr Dobbah. G. C. R. R. W. A. F. F.    Gunjur.
(Brikama) Central Kombo.    11/2/40

Sir,
I have the honour to draw you these few lines.
And I am also to ask you another favour to help me.
As I am still on Bed, I have got a very bad sore under
my private. & I wish you to get me (a medicine) that can
clean the dirt away, because its very dirt; So that
it can better more. I am fine that when you see the
complain of my sickness, you will be very sorry for
me & get me a good (Medicine) as I know you
love me well, as & how I love you?

(2) But please hi my good Master I am troubling very much
were I am. Will you be so kindly take my trouble to
do so hi?
I have the honour to be Sir.

Seyfu Mafody Tomay.
(Gunjur)
South Kombo

A letter to 'Major Dobbah' from the Seyfu of Gunjur, Mafody Tomay, asking for
help. The date is 1940, when the West African had complete faith in the 'white man'.

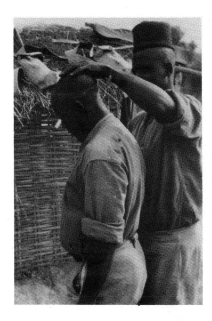

Baba Mafoli having a haircut.

Crossing a creek of the Gambia River.

**2nd Battalion Parachute Regiment, 1944.** *Back row:* Lieut. J. H. A. Monsell; Lieut. J. A. Russell; Lieut. A. Roberts; Lieut. A. L. Tannenbaum; Lieut. D. M. Douglass; Lieut. J. G. Blunt; Lieut. J. T. Ainslie; Lieut. J. G. Purdy; Lieut. A. J. McDermont; Lieut. R. A. Vlasto; Lieut. C. M. Stanford; Lieut. D. E. C. Russell; Lieut. G. F. W. Ellum. *Middle row:* Lieut. P. H. Cane; Capt. J. W. Logan, D.S.O., R.A.M.C.; Capt. A. Frank, M.C.; Lieut. J. H. Greyburn, V.C.; Lieut. W. N. Dormer; Lieut. P. H. Barry; Lieut. R. B. Woods; Capt. R. E. Morton; Lieut. R. H. Levien; Capt. J. Timothy, M.C.; Capt. A. J. Rutherford; Lieut. P. B. Jessop; Lieut. C. D. Briteux-Buchanan, M.C. *Front row:* Rev. B. M. Egan, M.C., C.F.(R.C.); Capt. D. McLean; Major V. Dover, M.C.; Major P. J. Albury; Major D. W. Wallis; Lieut.-Colonel J. D. Frost, D.S.O., M.C.; Major A. D. Tatham-Warter; Major D. E. Crawley, M.C.; Capt. F. K. Hoyer-Millar; Capt. S. C. Panter, M.C.; Lieut. (Qmr) J. T. Parker.

The portrait of Major-General John D. Frost which I painted in 1978 after he had retired from the army. I hope it reveals something of his cool, defiant attitude and the rock-like stance which inspired those who served under him in battle. His apparently sleepy eyes could flash with a suddenness that made a man move faster than he would have believed possible.

A rare aerial photograph of the railway bridge at Arnhem before the battle.

As we left the main road into the town of Arnhem the railway bridge seemed a long way away. The trees along the Polderweg gave cover during the early approach.

Nearer the bridge the cover afforded by the trees disappeared. In flat, open country like this the parachutist or infantry soldier feels very exposed—as indeed he is—to any enemy fire which may be covering the ground.

Photographs taken by the Dutch underground while the officers were waiting to escape from Arnhem: (*left*) Brigadier Gerald Lathbury (who on one occasion gave me 14 days' C.B.!) and (*right*) Major Digby Tatham-Warter, of umbrella fame.

## SPECIMEN MENU (GERMAN)

| | BREAKFAST | LUNCH | TEA | SUPPER |
|---|---|---|---|---|
| MON. | HOT WATER | PEA SOUP | ,, | BOILED POTATOES SAUERKRAUT. H.W. |
| TUES. | ,, | BOILED POTATOES | - | POTATOES. H.W. |
| WED. | ,, | BOILED MILLET | - | POTATOES COFFEE |
| THUR. | ,, | BOILED POTATOES | ,, | STEW |
| FRI. | ,, | HOT WATER | ,, | POTATOES COFFEE |
| SAT. | ,, | HOT WATER | ,, | POTATOES. H.W. |
| SUN. | - | BOILED POTATOES | ,, | POTATOES H.W |

The War Prisoners' Aid of the Y.M.C.A. issued prisoners with diaries in which meticulous records were often kept. As this page from my own diary shows, food became an obsession. I only received four half-boxes of Red Cross parcels during my eight months in Oflag 79, and not a single one of the many parcels sent from home.

## BULK WEEKLY ISSUE.

| | | |
|---|---|---|
| BREAD..... | 1½ LOAF | |
| MARG....... | ⅛ lb. | |
| CHEESE...... | 1/16 lb. | APPROX. |
| JAM ......... | 1/20 lb. | |
| SUGAR....... | ⅛ lb. | |

was to move from the dropping-zone and approach the town on the left flank to the north. The 3rd Battalion, commanded by Lieut.-Colonel Tony Fitch, was to advance in the centre, while the 2nd Battalion commanded by Lieut.-Colonel John Frost, would advance to the Arnhem road bridge direct by the way of the line of the river—the Neder Rijn.

It was the task of the 2nd Battalion, and particularly that of 'C' Company (the Company under my command) which mainly occupied my thoughts. We had our own 'three bridges' with which to contend: first, the railway bridge, second, the pontoon bridge and, finally, and most important—the road bridge.

The morning sunlight glistened on the wings of the aircraft. The sky was bright blue and the fields below were neat and orderly—England looked beautiful and it was difficult to believe that we were at war. When would we see her again? Here and there, small cottages snuggled among the woodlands and patch-work fields; in each one of them someone was surely cooking the Sunday (rationed) lunch—my family too, probably. Soon the coastline was left behind and the glistening water in the autumn sunlight was beneath us—we were now in neutral territory over the North Sea.

Looking down through the open doorway I saw a small convoy of little ships. There were a few M.T.B.s acting as escort, and the whole scene resembled toys deployed in a mimic battle.

By this time a fighter escort had joined the airborne armada; a fighter escort, especially when it was actually seen, was always very comforting—the Spitfires looked so efficient and so deter-mined. One pilot deliberately flew in close enough to wave from his cockpit, and as he peeled away he gave a quick lift of his hand with upturned thumb—then he was gone.

The misty coast of Europe was ahead. There is an exhilarating sense of trespassing when flying over hostile territory and a wave of supreme confidence surges through you knowing that in a few minutes you will descend from the sky and be upon an unsus-pecting enemy. A chink of uncertainty diminishes this confidence since there is always the possibility that the enemy may be lying in wait for you.

A stream of possibilities rushes through your mind. Will your 'chute open? Will your landing be a good one, or will you hit a tree, or a house, or break a leg—it's not good to be incapacitated on a dropping-zone! Will the enemy be firing across the dropping-zone? Will you land in the right place? Will you find the rendezvous and arrive at the right time? How many of your men will be with you at the rendezvous? If all goes well, will you have contact with Battalion Headquarters and learn that formations are complete and ready to move off? If the answers to all these doubts proved to be favourable, then only the battle would lie ahead. In my case, there was just one more thought—how long would my good luck last? Not for long, so it proved.

The floods in Holland were visible and it was difficult to distinguish between river and flooded land, but the Rhine was unmistakable as we flew over it; its gleaming waters quickly slid away. The red light above the door flickered—'Stand to the door!' The red light went out and the green light twinkled. It was the final signal—'GO!' Only the rushing sound of the slip-stream in your ears told you that you were airborne and on your way down. This was it!

The air was clean and as I oscillated in my parachute harness the horizon rose and dipped. As I descended I could see many figures on the dropping-zone moving about in all directions, but the most comforting sight was the huge cross of white tape which confirmed that we were at the right place.

My landing was comfortable, but an ammunition container was exploding a few yards to my right. I jettisoned my parachute and moved off in haste to the Company rendezvous. On the way I met my Company Sergeant-Major; it was a relief to see him—C.S.M. Tasker: he was the kind of soldier who had inspired Rudyard Kipling.

The time was now 14.45 hours. Two men of the Company had been injured on the dropping-zone—they had jumping injuries. It is never easy to give the order to move off when you have to leave casualties on a dropping-zone not knowing what their future fate may be.

The spare Bren gun carried by the Company was missing; all the light-weight motor cycles were damaged, and only one folding bicycle was in working order. The Company wireless set was in communication with Battalion headquarters for the first and what was to prove to be the only time.

I caught sight of Brigadier Lathbury, who waved. It was impossible to miss this man who was well over six feet tall, slim, and with a head which always reminded me of a handsome hungry eagle. He called out to me, 'You made it this time, Dicky.'

The 'drop' looked to be good and the troops swarming off the dropping-zone resembled a crowd leaving Twickenham on a Saturday afternoon at the end of a rugby international.

There appeared to be no immediate organized opposition, although firing could be heard on the far side of the dropping-zone. The explosions from a few burning containers were confusing. Civilians were running out from neighbouring farms to greet us. This was very reassuring, but it did not help since the British soldier is renowned for his ability to make friends—fraternization was no part of the operation at this stage.

'A' Company, commanded by Major Digby Tatham-Warter, of the Oxfordshire and Buckinghamshire Light Infantry, was to lead the advance of the 2nd Battalion to the road bridge. Digby was a cool, calm and collected man; he was tall, a little aloof and full of confidence. Little wonder that it was he who astonished the Germans by carrying an open umbrella during the battle. He made a brilliant escape from the bridge at Arnhem some days later. Years after the war he was found hidden away at Kilifi, forty miles from Mombasa in his adopted country, Kenya, running a safari company.

'C' Company was to capture the railway bridge, cross to the south bank and advance to the road bridge. If it was found impossible to cross the river by this bridge, then the Company was to enter the centre of the town and occupy the German headquarters building. 'B' Company, commanded by Major Doug Crawley, would follow 'A' Company after we had been committed to the railway bridge; they would proceed to the pontoon bridge and cross the river to the south side if we had been unsuccessful at the railway bridge. The Battalion would eventually form a tight defensive perimeter around the road bridge. The 1st and 3rd Battalions on our left flank would reinforce the perimeter. It all seemed simple, and flexible enough to succeed, particularly as the rest of the 1st Airborne Division would reinforce the initial assault by the 1st Brigade.

We were given the order to move off. I was worried because the 'walkie-talkies' were not working and the wireless set to Battalion H.Q. was faulty. Life becomes hell when wireless sets refuse to function and all the bad language in the world will not improve their performance.

I decided that I would have to move ahead with the leading platoon, so I left Captain Dicky Morton, my second-in-command, at the rear with Company H.Q. Dicky Morton was a very handsome officer, with a thick mop of wavy hair. He looked more like a man who was destined to make a career in films than a parachutist committed to battle. He had an old-world charm which he punctuated with flashes of fury.

Communication within the tight formation of the Company whilst on the move in daylight presented no problem, but it was already clear to me that when darkness fell control would become very difficult. We had little experience of fighting in built-up areas where it is easy to find yourself cut off, and without wireless communication command is very nearly impossible, as the Divisional Commander, Major-General Roy Urquhart, discovered before the battle was very old.

We reached the road leading east from Oosterbeek into Arnhem and the result of 'A' Company's first brush with the enemy was there for all to see. A Dutchman was dressing the wounds of four Germans—Luftwaffe personnel—and on the side of the road was a wrecked German staff car, with the occupants sprawled half in and half out of the vehicle. There is sometimes a sickening sympathy for the enemy when you see them past all further action and their bodies ripped and distorted. Subconsciously, perhaps you wonder how long it will be before your body lies on the ground never to move again.

The nearer our approach to the town the greater were our problems. The Dutch civilians were overjoyed to see us and assumed that for them the war was over. They joined in our advance in large numbers, which was a factor we had not foreseen. To be amongst friendly people in enemy-occupied territory, knowing full well that a bloody battle is imminent, does not help the concentration of the commander or the commanded. It was all so unreal—this mixture of friendliness and impending fury.

A Dutchman who spoke splendid English insisted on walking beside me with his bicycle. He was in a great state of jubilation and wished to accompany us into the town where he imagined a great welcome would be awaiting us. He was quite right, but the welcome was not of the kind he had in mind. This man remained with the Company until the very end when he was shot out of hand by the Germans.

The outskirts of Arnhem are much like the outskirts of any English county town. Houses and smallholdings are scattered about and there is an abundance of woodland. Autumn was near and the trees were turning brown and gold. There was no sign of the war. Perhaps this operation was going to be merely an exercise in occupation with a few minor brushes with rear German troops. Perhaps!

The approach march was about eight miles, too long, I thought, if it was necessary to gain surprise. Perhaps there was nothing very much on the ground to surprise. Perhaps!

It was now about 5 o'clock in the afternoon. John Frost gave permission for 'C' Company to move off to the right flank for the assault on the railway bridge. This could now be seen very clearly and was much larger than I had imagined from the photographs at the briefing. It stood out clearly against the sky—very exposed it seemed to me. There was no cover to its approach. As we left the Battalion column and moved down the small track lined by stumped trees—the Polderweg—I looked over my shoulder and watched 'A' Company leading the Battalion into the town. I could not help but wonder when we would link up again.

There were ack-ack positions north and south of the railway bridge manned by Reichsdeutscher who were personnel who had for the greater part of their lives lived in Holland. These positions had been previously manned by the Arbeitsdienst—Hitler Youth—who had been moved elsewhere the day before our assault. There was also a permanent guard on the bridge itself consisting of ten men under the command of a Feldwebel. They were billeted in an inn close by—the Koeweide.

The importance of bridge guards had not been overlooked by the local German commander, Field Marshal Model. On 16 September, the day before our arrival on the scene, he had issued a communication which stated: 'The manner in which bridges are now guarded requires thorough revision. There must be no more scenes of soldiers standing guard on a bridge surrounded by civilians. A tight security ring will be thrown around all bridges. Barriers will be erected where necessary. The bridge security detachment must be posted adjacent to or under the bridge. Civilian traffic will be directed across bridges in controlled lots.

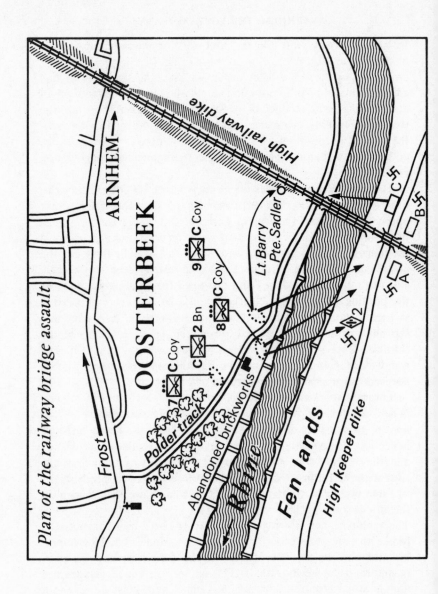

Plan of the railway bridge assault

ARNHEM →

OOSTERBEEK

High railway dike

C Coy
9 C Coy
8 C Coy
2 Bn
1 C Coy
7 C Coy

Lt. Barry
Pte. Sadler

C
B
A

2

Frost

Polder track

Abandoned brickworks

Rhine

Fen lands

High keeper dike

Demolition parties will take up positions in the immediate vicinity of the bridges. Guards will ensure the rapid alerting of demolition crews. Mine obstacles which can be installed speedily must be kept at hand.'

The Polderweg along which we made our way was little more than a track. There was no cover and we were exposed to fire from the far side of the river.

Number 9 Platoon was in the lead, followed by Company H.Q. and 8 and 7 Platoons. The German positions in a brick kiln on the north side of the river had been heavily bombed by the R.A.F. and most of the buildings had been demolished. The opposition to our approach was light and was quickly overrun. 9 Platoon continued its advance to the railway bridge without trouble until they reached the foot of the escarpment of the railway track itself. Here it came under heavy fire from a machine-gun and from snipers on the far side of the river. The remainder of the Company took up covering fire positions in the area of the wrecked buildings.

Lieut. Peter Barry, the Platoon Commander, deployed two sections on the ground to give close covering fire while he with the third section climbed up to the bridge under cover of smoke. It was a model attack and all seemed to be going well. Our covering fire silenced the opposition on the far bank. Peter with his assaulting section reached the first span of the bridge and started to cross. When they were a third of the way over there was a yellow flash and a tremendous explosion. The Spreng-kommando and his henchman could be seen running from the far side of the bridge, and they only just made it before the centre span sank into the river with the railway lines draping down like reeds into the water.

From my position at Company H.Q. I could see Peter's men on the bridge running back, dragging two of the section with them. There was no wireless communication so I had to go forward on foot with my batman to find out how badly the section had been hit and if there was any chance of crossing the river by other means than the bridge. As we arrived at the escarpment, Private Sadler of 9 Platoon came down the embankment towards us. He did not deliver his message: he dropped dead from a sniper's bullet before he reached us. It was at this moment that I began to feel that fortune was not smiling on us although the sun was bright.

From the base of one of the pillars of the bridge I was able, above the noise of the firing which had now increased, to order the section to withdraw. I shouted out to Peter to come down and see me. He called back, 'I can't move, sir, I've been hit.' From the sound of his voice I knew that he was in a bad way. Peter was a fearless leader with the confidence of ten ordinary men; it was this belief that he had a charmed life which led him to comment more than once that there were no Germans good enough to check any advance he made with his Platoon. Over the months before Arnhem I had listened to this young man's confidence and learned to share it. That we had lost him so early in the battle came as a shock. I swore loudly and long.

Corporal Roberts, the Company medical orderly, was left with Peter with instructions to stay with him and if possible to move him to a local hospital. Roberts did a good job. Peter Barry survived his wounds and Roberts eventually escaped back to England.

The strange nagging feeling that things were not going as planned became stronger. A handful of men had prevented us from crossing the bridge. Would the same thing happen at the pontoon bridge and at the main road bridge? When I returned to Company H.Q. I sensed that the men were beginning to share my concern. They were old campaigners and could 'smell' the course of battle. If anything, this stiffened their determination. None the less, the Battalion was now out of sight; we had no wireless communication with John Frost or any of the other Companies and indeed we were very much on our own.

In the book *By Air To Battle*, it is stated that Lieut. Peter Barry and his Platoon were accompanied to the railway bridge by a section of Royal Engineers of the 9th Field Company under command of Captain E. O'Callaghan. This was not so; Lieut. Peter Stainforth, R.E., was in command of the sappers attached to 'C' Company, and they did not take part in the assault on the bridge. Peter Stainforth's own account in *Wings of the Wind* makes the position clear: his job was to stand by and clear the bridge of demolition charges after it had been captured. In the event his task was done for him by the Germans!

The situation was now very different from that which had prevailed half an hour before. The bridge was lost and it was not possible to cross to the other bank. No boats were in sight. The Company was deployed and under fire. We were out of touch with everyone, except the Germans.

I decided to re-form the Company and move back as quickly as possible along the Polderweg to the main road and make for our second objective—the German Headquarters in the centre of the town. Just where it was we did not know, but we would soon find out. The Polderweg was the only line of withdrawal since the route across the open fields was exposed to fire from the Germans on the far side of the river. It was a long way round and would lose time, but it was safer. I had already lost too many men and the battle had only just started—if there was to be a battle.

As we withdrew, I received a verbal message from Major David Wallace, the second-in-command of the Battalion. The runner told me that I must proceed to my second objective and that a jeep and further orders would be waiting for me when I reached the main road. This was good news. If I could get my hands on a jeep I could go forward and make a reconnaissance before committing the Company.

John Frost, obviously, had seen what had happened and wanted me to continue with the alternative plan—to move into the town and capture the German Headquarters. I presumed that Doug Crawley with his Company would now attempt to cross the river by way of the pontoon bridge. The messenger also told me that I was to leave Peter Stainforth and his sappers in the area to ensure that no further damage to the railway bridge took place. From where I stood it did not appear possible to do very much more anyway.

We arrived at the main road glad to be out of range of the snipers who were still potting at us from the far bank of the river. I found no jeep waiting for me and no one to give me any further message. The Company wireless set was still refusing to function.

We were just about to continue our move along the road which would take us into the centre of the town when I saw the Brigade Staff Captain coming down the road behind us. He had three or four men with him. I stopped and asked him if he knew anything about the general situation. He replied, 'As far as I can tell, we have jumped into a grand military cock-up! The 3rd Battalion have been held up and are laagering for the night. The 1st Battalion have run into heavy opposition and are held up as well. The 2nd Battalion are moving towards the road bridge, as far as I know. Brigade and Divisional Headquarters seem to have vanished off the face of the earth. There is no wireless contact.' I thanked him and decided that we must move on as fast as we could.

Perhaps the situation was not as bad as it sounded. The Germans may have misread the purpose and pattern of the attack and committed all their strength against the 1st and 3rd Battalions, leaving us a free hand to make the road bridge.

The light was fading and our second objective was at least a mile further on. The Dutchman with a bicycle was still with us and he seemed to be oblivious of my growing concern. The men would want some rest before the night was out, but there was no question of taking a breather at the moment. They were also getting hungry, but again there was no question of halting for a brew-up. We just had to push on, but to where?

Our advance continued into the town with 8 Platoon leading, followed by Company H.Q., 7 Platoon and the depleted 9 Platoon. The open country came to an abrupt end. We were now moving down a main road with buildings on both sides. There were few breaks between the houses and few doorways or openings in which to take cover should the necessity arise. I hoped that if we could make good speed we would reduce the distance between Battalion H.Q. and ourselves and this would increase the chances of regaining wireless contact.

The whole Company was now stretched out and astride the road—Utrechtseweg, which changed its name to Utrechtsestraat as it entered the centre of the town. As the light faded our pace slowed down, tension and tiredness were creeping up upon us.

I was with the leading Platoon when it happened. Ian Russell, was the commander of that Platoon, a Scot who had not seen action before. He was to become a veteran before the battle was over. We saw just ahead of us a group of Germans lined up in threes at the side of the road. They were standing at ease, but had rifles with them. Our first instinct was to halt the Company. These Germans were silent and gave us the impression that they had been taken prisoner. Why we should have come to this immediate conclusion I cannot imagine, but we did.

John Frost might have changed his mind and made his approach to the road bridge by way of the centre of the town and these were prisoners taken during that advance. If not, why were they just standing there as if on parade?

I shouted out for the Battalion I.O., 'Bucky' Boiteux-Buchanan, whose responsibility they would be. 'Bucky! Bucky! What the hell are these Germans doing with their rifles?' There was no reply, but

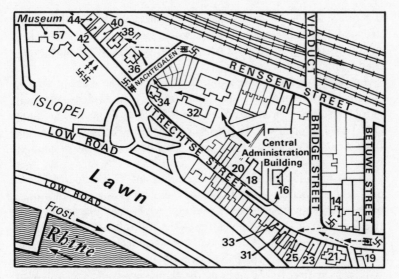

This drawing shows the point where the main body of the 2nd Battalion took the tow-path on the north river bank while 'C' Company took the main road, Utrecht Street, into the centre of the town of Arnhem. It also shows the dispositions of 'C' Company at the time of the massacre of the German troops outside St Elizabeth Hospital.

the ranks of the Germans began to shuffle. Suddenly the penny dropped—these Germans were not prisoners, they had just de-bussed from two vehicles which could be seen at the side of the road behind them.

Ian and I came to the same conclusion at the same time and simultaneously leapt off the road and into a garden—the only garden in sight. Ian shouted for the P.I.A.T.s (Projectors Infantry anti-Tank) to open up. 'Kill those bloody Huns before they kill us. For Christ's sake hurry! Fire, Fire!' Two Bren guns also opened up before he had finished shouting.

What magnificent men were these Scots of 'C' Company. It was only seconds before P.I.A.T. bombs were exploding into the midst of the Germans. There were about eighty of them and by the time five bombs had landed only a few were still interested in the war. Bodies were flung in all directions, the wounded were moaning and one of the vehicles, which had presumably brought them to this spot, caught fire. In the light of the flames we could see just what we had done. It was a very unpleasant sight. Strangely enough this action took place outside St Elizabeth Hospital, but I fear that most of those Germans were beyond the help of that or any other hospital. Three came towards us and surrendered; two of them were wounded.

Lieut. David Russell, who commanded 7 Platoon, spoke German and he ascertained from our captives that there were no other British forces in the town. He was told that the airborne attack was a failure and that German troops would soon round us all up. These Germans were very arrogant even though they were now prisoners. I believe they thought that they would not be prisoners for very long, and they were right. They also told David that they were only part of an advance party and that armoured vehicles were guarding the centre of the town. In spite of the fact that many of their German comrades lay dying, they seemed to be quite indifferent to their plight. We did not then know that Field Marshal Walter Model had the situation well in hand, in spite of mistakes made by one of his junior commanders, Major Sepp Krafft of the S.S. Panzer Grenadier Training and Reserve Battalion. We also did not know that it was to be Lieut.-Colonel Walter Harzer who was to concentrate his strength on the two main highways into Arnhem: the Ede–Arnhem road and the Utrecht–Arnhem road—we were now astride the latter.

In his book *A Bridge Too Far* Cornelius Ryan records: 'By oversight, or perhaps because he lacked sufficient forces at the moment, Harzer failed to position any groups along a quiet secondary road running parallel to the northern bank of the Rhine. It was the single unprotected route the British could take to the Arnhem bridge.' This was the route by which John Frost had chosen to take the 2nd Battalion.

There can be little doubt that Harzer was well pleased with his defensive counter-attack. He had only to find the 2nd Battalion and the battle was over. When he encountered 'C' Company on Utrechtsestraat, in spite of the losses he initially suffered outside St Elizabeth Hospital, he thought that he had found the advance guard of the 2nd Battalion, when in fact John Frost was making his way to the Arnhem bridge without opposition.

At this time John Frost realized that his main threat came from his left flank 'Den Brink' and sent Doug Crawley to deal with the opposition on the high ground, leaving the rest of the Battalion a clear run. Doug was successful, but he lost one of his ace junior commanders—Peter Cane. This attack also helped to convince the Germans that the advance of the 2nd Battalion was down Utrechtsestraat.

There was no point in hanging about, we had to press on regardless of the shambles we had created. We had suffered no casualties from this encounter.

The Company was soon on the move again. Time had been lost and it was now quite dark. As the Company made its way forward I had a strong feeling that we were advancing into a blind alley. The houses were very close and none of them had lights showing; there was no chance to change course—it felt like marching down a black tunnel. The absolute silence, except for the sound of crunching boots on the road, was eerie.

Ian Russell was still leading the advance with his Platoon and I remained by his side only a few yards behind the leading scouts. Something was bound to happen sooner or later—and it happened almost at once.

The silence and the darkness were abruptly shattered by long bursts from three machine-guns to our immediate front. Tracer bullets flew off the surface of the road and ricochets were bouncing off the walls of the houses. It looked as though we had suddenly walked into a Chinese fire-cracker festival—the sparks from the

95

tracer bullets and ricochets seemed to be all around us. The two leading scouts were hit and fell in the middle of the road. The Company took what cover it could in the doorways of the buildings. We were no longer in a black tunnel, but in a tunnel lit with a thousand sparks.

I could see that there was one house a little way forward and to our left which had a small garden. I called back to David Russell to move the Company forward to this garden during the lulls in the firing. Thank God all guns have to be reloaded!

Just how the Company eventually assembled in the confined area of this garden I shall never know. There were nearly a hundred men in the space of a two-storey house and its small plot, no larger than thirty yards by twenty yards, thankfully surrounded by a brick wall. Eventually, we managed to extend the area by occupying the building of the Central Administration, No. 16, as well as house No. 18.

Company H.Q. was in the house (No. 18) and the remainder were organized into all-round defensive positions. In the darkness it was nearly impossible to ensure that we had protection from every line of approach. Time had passed quickly, but the men were tired. They had been up since early morning, had had no food and had marched the best part of ten miles and been engaged in two minor clashes with the enemy.

Sentries were posted for the night and I ordered the men to get as much rest as they could, for there was surely to be a major engagement on the following morning. Having stopped us, I did not think that the Germans would commit themselves until first light since they could see no more than we. Meanwhile, we continued to try and contact Battalion H.Q. on the wireless set.

During the night our hopes rose when we made contact with Support Company who had reached the area of the pontoon bridge which we were led to believe existed. I spoke later to Doug Crawley who had also reached the pontoon bridge area. I learned that he could not cross the river at this point because no pontoon bridge existed and that both he and Support Company were proceeding to the main road bridge to join Johnny Frost and the rest of the Battalion. I told Doug that I was pinned down and would not be able to move until just before first light; at that time I would double back and make my way with the Company to the tow-path by the river and attempt to reach the bridge by that route—there seemed to be little value in advancing into the town which was obviously defended by a far stronger force. In the circumstances Colonel John would want me at the road bridge. Doug agreed and said he would pass on the message of my intentions.

This contact was reassuring, but we were still unable to establish a link direct to Battalion H.Q.; my conversation with Doug Crawley was the last time the wireless functioned.

House No. 18 was occupied by a Dutchman, Rinia van Nauta, and his family. This poor man, his wife and children found themselves on a warm Sunday evening suddenly trapped in their home and surrounded by parachutists. It was a beautiful house, splendidly furnished and certainly not intended to be a fortress for troops with hobnailed boots. Rinia van Nauta was a kind and very helpful soul, difficult traits to maintain when his home was being torn apart. Windows were being knocked in and his furniture was being piled up to form barricades.

His greatest anxiety, naturally, was the safety of his family. I do not believe that anyone can appreciate the extent of the pain of such a situation unless they have had personal experience; to be caught in the middle of a battle with your family around you is the worst kind of horror. Rinia van Nauta was a brave man, but however hard he tried to conceal his feelings the anguish in his eyes was plain to see. The British soldier, although I doubt if he would admit it, is a very sentimental creature and considerate to those who are defenceless—including prisoners-of-war. There was not a man in the Company who did not feel concern and share some of the anguish of this Dutchman. War is madness gone mad!

The night passed reasonably quietly. Only a few random shots were fired by the Germans—a ploy to keep the troops awake and their nerves on edge. At first light we all knew that the Germans would attack, probably with armoured vehicles since we had heard the sound of their tracks. I suggested to Rinia van Nauta that it would be better if he and his family left the house and moved away from what was bound to become a battle area. He told me that he had friends in a house which was not far away; perhaps they would be safer there. The risk of moving back along the route which we had taken would be less than waiting for the battle which was certain to come. In the darkness such a small party could move without being heard, especially if they removed their shoes. I agreed to send two soldiers with him for protection should he run into trouble; if things took a turn for the worse they could always return to the Company area. In truth I was not sure that this was a good idea, but I could not face the prospect of having this family in our midst on the morrow. I was prepared to take the risk and allowed them to leave with the two escorts. In the event it proved to be a good move. They made contact with their friends, the two escorts returned safely and the following morning the Germans made their expected attack. I do not think that Rinia van Nauta and his family would have stood very much chance of surviving that attack—their house eventually caught fire.

It is not difficult to imagine the atmosphere and the feelings of the inhabitants of Utrechtsestraat during that night. Arnhem was occupied territory, but most of the residents were living in their own homes, although some had been requisitioned by the Germans. Before the war, a number of residents of the Straat had been Jewish. For example, the house on the corner of Bridge Street was a raincoat factory owned by the brothers Roos. They had been put in a concentration camp and the factory was now occupied by a German Verwalter, but he had made his disappearance immediately on hearing of the airborne landings.

The Orphanage was the H.Q. of the Luftwaffe and was occupied as such until the morning of our arrival, but receiving the news of parachute landings the building was evacuated in some haste. It was used as a radio station and there was on the roof a kind of radar antenna reputed to serve installations at the border of Holland and Germany.

No. 15 was believed to be the H.Q. of the local Gestapo. This building was also evacuated on the afternoon of 17 September. The Town Major, Major General Kussin, had his H.Q. at Nieuwe Plein.

No. 25 was the Hotel Busseraud, owned by Mr Schwamer. It was used as a dormitory for the Luftwaffe and there also were installed a *Zahlmeister* (Administration Officer), clerks and a cook. Some local girls were employed to do the domestic chores. Next door, at No. 23, was housed a Nazi press photographer, Gazendedenk. The Germans had decamped from all these premises shortly after midday on 17 September.

At the north-west corner of Bridge Street were premises occupied by a greengrocer. They had been taken over by the

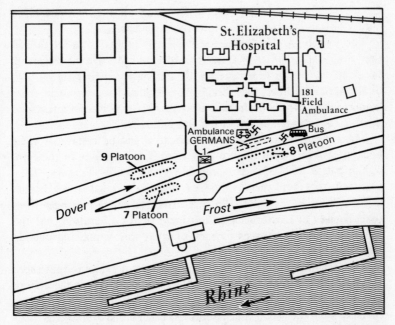

The withdrawal of 'C' Company over the high walls of houses, numbers 18 to 30. The final stand was made in houses numbered 38, 40, 42 and 43.

Germans as a temporary dressing-station. Opposite, at the eastern corner of the street, was an estate agent's house.

The foregoing gives some idea of the civilians in the area and the situation when we arrived. Most of the Dutch residents heralded the airborne invasion with delight when first they heard of it. Here was liberation! Some had decided to stay put in their homes, while others preferred to move out to places of presumed greater safety until the liberation was assured.

Many of the Dutch people, barricaded in the cellars of their houses, emerged from time to time to obtain some idea of the state of the battle. No. 33 was occupied by the family Verkerk. They gathered together their valuables and barricaded their house, taking refuge in the cellar. They received telephone messages from their friends in Oosterbeek telling them of the liberation, but the Verkerks had reservations in view of what was happening outside their own house.

The Germans entered Nos. 33 and 31 and, presuming that there were parachute troops upstairs in No. 31, shot through the ceiling with their automatic weapons. After the battle, in the garden, covered by some wood and rubbish, Verkerk discovered a British Army pay-book wrapped up in a piece of cloth. This book belonged to Sergeant William Burns, who was reported 'missing' at Arnhem. He had managed to cross the road early in the battle, but later was trapped in the garden of this house and lost his life. Sergeant Burns's record is both remarkable and significant. He had enlisted at Berwick in 1940, was taken prisoner in Italy but escaped; he returned to England badly wounded, and could have withdrawn from active service. Instead, he volunteered to rejoin the 2nd Battalion to take part in operation 'Market Garden'. In civilian life, he was an artist and something of an idealist. After the war ended Verkerk made an attempt to return the pay-book to Burns's next-of-kin, but found that she, his mother, had emigrated to America to join her sister. A friend of the Burns family returned the pay-book to Verkerk as a souvenir.

The Dutch gradually realized that the battle was going against the British airborne troops. More and more the Germans were gaining strength, and more and more armoured vehicles were moving into position. House after house was being occupied by German troops. A column of tanks was stationed in Brugstraat and a heavy machine-gun was sighted at the northern end of this street on the railway embankment, camouflaged behind a parapet.

So was the background of some of the people with whom we were enmeshed. To fight an armed enemy is one thing, but to be involved with civilians in a confined area, civilians who were both friendly and frightened, is another matter.

The three prisoners whom we had taken outside St Elizabeth Hospital and our own wounded were kept in the cellar of the house No. 18, together with Company H.Q. personnel. The dead had been carried from the road and lay covered on the floor. Unlike an infantry battalion, we had no line of communication to a Regimental Aid Post, and you cannot bury your dead in the middle of a town.

At about 3 o'clock in the morning I walked round the Company area. The sentries were alert: David and Ian had kept them on their toes. Few men were actually asleep and they seemed in very good heart and remarkably calm in view of what they would have to face in a few hours' time. It was while I was making this round that I was hit in the backside with something; exactly what it was I shall never know. One thing is certain: a piece of metal entered one cheek and made its exit the other side and then entered the second cheek and made its final exit. Four small holes through the cheeks of my rump.

The soldier with me said, 'What's up, sir?' as I clutched at the slight sting at my rear end. There was a trickle of blood. I dropped my trousers while my companion wiped and dressed the small wounds. As he did so he gave me some encouragement, with the comment, 'Sir, you'll get your discharge with this one. You'll be no bloody good in the Army, but the Navy will have you—you've got five of 'em!' The humour of the soldier is frequently lewd, but unquenchable in times of stress.

Before first light I gave the orders for a withdrawal. The Company would retrace its steps by the way of the back-gardens of the houses, cross Utrechtsestraat in the area of the Museum and make for the low road by the river. They would then proceed with all haste to the road bridge and link up with the remainder of the Battalion.

This plan might have been possible but for three factors: one, we did not know that all the walls joining the gardens were ten feet high; two, we did not know that the whole area was covered by sniper-fire from the buildings overlooking the gardens, and, last but not least, we did not know that there was an underground passage linking the two sides of Utrechtsestraat.

As the Company withdrew, with 7 Platoon leading, the men had to climb over wall after wall with their heavy equipment while snipers were active. These walls slowed down the pace of the withdrawal and lost us the surprise of a sudden departure, which had been our intent. The houses overlooking the gardens had an unrestricted view of us and the windows exposed many peering faces. We did not fire because we were unable to distinguish friend from foe.

The Germans soon reacted to the slowness of our withdrawal. Half-track vehicles kept abreast with us along Utrechtsestraat and snipers seemed to be everywhere. The Company did well in the circumstances until it came to a narrow road linking Utrechtsestraat and the railway line. This was Nightingale Walk (Nachtegalspad) which was covered by automatic fire from the railway embankment.

The trap was set—and we were walking into it. There was no alternative and no way out. The only consolation was that we were keeping a lot of Germans away from the road bridge. Unless we could cross to the far side of the road and reach the river it would only be a matter of time before the armour closed in and destroyed us. The noise of the armoured vehicles in the confined area was magnified by the crunch of shells which the Germans were now firing into the buildings on our immediate left. The German soldier is a good soldier; anyone who thinks differently does not know him, and he knew exactly what we were trying to do and he also knew that he had the weapons to stop us. A confident German soldier is a very formidable enemy.

There were iron railings on the far side of Nightingale Walk and the last of the P.I.A.T. bombs were used to blast a hole in them—these spiked railings were likely to be more formidable than the brick walls. Smoke bombs were fired to conceal our crossing and Sergeant Campbell, on his own initiative, took up a position in house No. 34. He hurled grenades at the armoured vehicles in Utrechtsestraat and in retaliation the Germans fired incendiary shells into the house, which soon became a blazing inferno.

The smoke which had been put down was thickened by that

from the burning buildings and under its black cloak Lieut. David Russell attempted to cross Utrechtsestraat at the road junction with one of his sections. This was a brave but disastrous decision. Three of the section were hit by fire from the railway embankment and the remainder were left on the far side of the road, cut off. David and his men were in the area of the burning house, No. 34, when I last saw them.

After the war, David explained what happened. 'We had just emerged from a small garden which opened on to Nightingale Walk when the Germans started firing with 20mm. flak into the house which we had just left. The firing felt uncomfortable coming from behind, but even worse when a quick look round told us that they had the road on a fixed line from the railway embankment and were opening up with Schmeissers on the far side of the house. Victor had said push on, so we climbed over yet another wall and started to crawl along the side of a house screened by low rose bushes. I ordered the section I had with me to make a dash for it. They hurled themselves across the road and down the bank on the other side. M.G.s and snipers opened up on them. It didn't seem a good idea to try and cross from the same spot, so I crawled on with another section. When we reached the end of the rose-bed I gave the signal to Sergeant Campbell who had just left a burning house, and ran myself to the far side of Utrechtsestraat, the bullets fairly cracking round. Once over the bank, I found myself in the midst of the section which had previously crossed: Sergeant Fleming, Lance-Corporal Vernon, Privates Vale, McKernon, Spicer and Cockburn. Neither Sergeant Campbell nor anyone else followed me. I assumed Campbell had been hit.'

Ian Russell then attempted to break out and cross the road. He, with one of his sections, disappeared into the smoke and they were not seen again.

The situation had rapidly deteriorated. In addition to the loss of Peter Barry I had now probably lost my other two platoon commanders. Without any form of communication and surrounded by brick walls and buildings, to say nothing of the Germans, the Company was disintegrating. Company H.Q. and the remnants of the three platoons took up defensive positions in houses Nos. 38 and 40. There were now only 25 men under my direct command. The rest were scattered on the far side of Utrechtsestraat and out of sight.

The trap was closing. The enemy was bringing his armoured vehicles closer since he realized that we had no weapons which could do them any harm. 20mm. shells were fired into the two houses which we occupied—we had nothing with which to retaliate except small arms. It was like shooting peas at a barn door. Both houses filled with smoke and it was becoming difficult to breathe.

A number of commanders, at different levels, have had to face the realization that the battle in which they are engaged is not going in their favour and that defeat is inevitable. Those who have never lost a battle are fortunate because they have not had to face the decision whether to fight to the last man and the last round, or whether to surrender—and just when. To surrender is a humiliating experience in any circumstance, to fight to the last man and the last round can be, but is not always, an abortive waste of lives. Whatever conclusion a commander reaches in these circumstances, he will for ever question himself as to whether he made the right decision. History will reach its own conclusions—it is so much easier to write history than to make it. Only those who have had to make such a decision to surrender can fully appreciate the depths of despair which accompany it.

There were a number of wounded stranded across the road. We could hear them calling for help. It was now not possible to reach them.

In the circumstances the men were very steady. They knew that this was a battle they would not and could not win. For a time the firing ceased and it seemed as though the Germans were taking a breather, but the pause was soon followed by a new threat—incendiaries were brought to the fore—adding fuel to the buildings already burning. The area was now alight.

I made the decision. 'Cease firing!'

In what is now called Airborne House, the remnants of 'C' Company made their last stand.

I had never seriously given a thought to the possibility of being taken prisoner and cannot describe what the first moments of capture are like, but every prisoner-of-war knows. The knowledge of failure and that there is to be no second chance is difficult to accept. I was conscious of the wounded about me, including Germans.

The only Dutch personnel in No. 38—the house where we now

stood—were the caretaker, Bokhoven, and his son. In due course, Bokhoven was taken prisoner by the Germans and put into a concentration camp in Germany, where he died. Young Bokhoven, however, survived.

What subsequently happened at Airborne House after 'C' Company was overwhelmed is obscure. Lieut.-Colonel Boeree, a Dutchman, carried out a detailed investigation into the part played by the 2nd Battalion, South Staffordshire Regiment, at Arnhem. He came to the conclusion that 'A' Company of this Battalion reached the middle building of the Provincial Electricity Company. The mortar group—under the command of Captain Willcocks and Lieut. Reynolds—advanced still further and occupied No. 38. This is borne out by the fact what when Superintendent Panhuyzen of the Provincial Electricity Company had an opportunity of going through the house after the battle, he found there the 'Signal Register' of the Mortar Group (Army Book No. 156), containing a list of the names and numbers of the personnel and the names and addresses of their next-of-kin. A copy was discovered in Capt. Willcocks's folder of the confidential 'Pocket Book of the German Army, 1943, Amendments No. 2'. There is no doubt that some South Staffordshire men were for a time in Airborne House.

Panhuyzen's conclusions were that the Germans left No. 38 after we had been overwhelmed, and that British troops (undoubtedly Captain Willcocks and his mortar detachment of the South Staffordshire Regiment) later again took possession, and held it for more than an hour. These were the same group of men who for a time had entered and who were obliged to evacuate the building of the Provincial Electricity Company, and then stood their ground 'pressed to the west wall of the building before retreating in a westerly direction'. Elements of the South Staffordshire Regiment penetrated almost, but not quite, as far into the town of Arnhem as did 'C' Company. The honour of claiming Airborne House—a matter of some pride as well as interest historically—is shared between 'C' Company, 2nd Battalion, 1st Parachute Brigade, and the Mortar Group, 2nd Battalion, South Staffordshire Regiment.

Ian and David Russell, both having been cut off from the Company, fought their own private battles for a further two days, gradually withdrawing. Ian Russell received a wound which temporarily blinded him and his gallantry in action was recognized later by His Majesty. Both these splendid young officers were captured and made prisoners until the end of the war. How hard they fought on their own and without any knowledge of the progress of the main battle.

Out of a great failure, I like to feel that the men of 'C' Company, who suffered a great deal in so short a time, delayed the great pressure which subsequently came upon those who reached the main road bridge at Arnhem. There can be no doubt that those who did reach that bridge made for themselves and for British military history a chapter of unsurpassed valour.

From the area of the fighting, in the days immediately following, some of the 'natives' evacuated themselves. Many of their houses had been fired and the great majority of these were very badly damaged. Moreover, the attitude of the Germans was decidedly uncertain. The fact that the Dutch had at times seen some of them in a state bordering on panic did not help. The Hollanders were suspected—often with justification—to have gone out of their way to encourage and support their would-be 'liberators'.

The Germans decided to evacuate the civil population, not only of Arnhem, but also of Oosterbeek, Wolfhezen, Heelsum, Renkum, Wageningen and Rhenen, and later, Bennekom also, a total of some 200,000 inhabitants. An impression at one time existed that this was a punitive measure, but it would appear to have been decided upon in the light of military exigencies. The reasoning of the Germans was that the British landing at Arnhem had failed in its purpose; but the Allies had established a bridgehead north of Nijmegen, and their thrust was becoming more powerful each day. The Siegfried Line ended at Nijmegen. The Germans were conscious of a possible further attack on that flank. Accordingly, they decided to fortify a dual line as a corridor. One line coincided with the River Ijssel running northwards from Arnhem; the other was the Grebbe line of defence, running from the Rhine northward, west of Wageningen. Both lines reached to the Zuider Zee. The northern bank of the Rhine was brought into a state of defence and this necessitated the evacuation of the civil population.

The whole population of Arnhem—some 100,000 souls—was instructed on Sunday, 24 September 1944, to evacuate their town at short notice. Men, women and children were ordered to pack up and get out, carrying away no more of their effects than they could porter themselves. Everything else they owned had to be left behind. As a reprisal, the German troops were then authorized to loot all the premises, an instruction which was obeyed with great thoroughness. The fugitives were supplied with no transport whatsoever, irrespective of age or fitness to travel.

They marched in a long column along the road to Apeldoorn. On the journey they were sighted by five American planes, which mistook them for a German column on the move and strafed them. The horrors of this evacuation remain as firmly in the memory of the people of Arnhem as their excitement at the premature news that their freedom was on the way through operation 'Market Garden'.

The Germans had halted the 1st and 3rd Battalions and, looking back, one is bound to wonder what would have happened had they realized that the main advance of the 2nd Battalion was along the north river bank and not, as they no doubt originally thought, along Utrechtsestraat where 'C' Company was engaged and subsequently overrun. When the Germans discovered their mistake the main body of the 2nd Battalion had reached and taken possession of the main road bridge at Arnhem.

Cornelius Ryan in *A Bridge Too Far* records: 'Frost had sent Major Douglas Crawley's "B" Company to the high ground above the nearby railway embankment with anti-tank guns to protect the battalion's left flank, freeing "A" Company to dash for the bridge.'

A footnote adds, 'As Frost recalls, "a map I had taken from a German prisoner ... showed the routes of an enemy armoured car patrol unit and I realized that the German strength was to my left".' This supports the contention that the Germans originally and mistakenly took 'C' Company to be the advance guard of the 2nd Battalion.

I believe that there were many factors which decided the fate of Arnhem, but there were two major ones: the presence, by chance, of German 'armour' at the right place and the right time sealed the fate of the 'infantry' airborne. Although the Germans had no prior knowledge of the attack, their reaction was immediate. Perhaps at this stage of the war the British higher command was over-confident and took too little notice of intelligence reports. However, General Sir Brian Horrocks, who commanded 30 Corps, decided to continue to advance with armour after the Nijmegen bridge had been captured, an advance which did not reach its objective—the bridge. The route was covered by German guns and there was no room for manoeuvre. Had an advance been made earlier and to a flank with a supported infantry division the link might have been possible, in spite of everything. Supported infantry, moving to a flank in the early stages of the battle, might have stood a very good chance of relieving the pressure. After twenty-four hours it was too late, the errors had been made, including the maxim 'never reinforce failure'.

Lieut.-Colonel Boeree, who lived at Arnhem at the time of the battle, wrote in *The Battle of Arnhem* as follows:

'It is usual to praise victorious troops for their heroism. But the story of Arnhem and Oosterbeek is of a feat of arms in which the protagonists were faced with unexpected reverses practically from the start. They died in their hundreds; the seriously wounded were taken to emergency hospitals, which were short of everything. As they were completely surrounded, it was impossible to evacuate the wounded, as is normally done.

'It was in these circumstances that the British showed what superb soldiers they were. The more deeply we go into the details of this battle the more admiration we feel for their courage, their typical sang-froid, their good morale, their comradeship and above all their splendid discipline, a discipline which had not been imposed upon them from above, as was the case with the Germans on the other side of the perimeter, but which emanated from the men themselves.'

Nearly thirty-three years later, on 16 June 1977, I attended a private viewing of the film based on the book by Cornelius Ryan with the title *A Bridge Too Far*. I had enjoyed reading the book and had exchanged correspondence with the author, whom I greatly admired. I had looked forward to seeing the film for many months, not that I wished to relive the Arnhem engagement, but because I wanted to see if it was possible to produce a clear picture of the complicated pattern of this famous battle for the three bridges which crossed the Maas, the Waal and the Lower Rhine.

Sir Richard Attenborough, the Director of the film, had kindly written to me on 17 May 1976; in his letter he said, 'For copyright reasons our script is based entirely on the material contained within Cornelius Ryan's book. Indeed one of the major problems has been to condense the vast amount of research he amassed into three hours of screen time. It is my fervent hope, however, that the finished production will not only be worthy of those who fought so bravely, but will also provide an overall understanding of this tragic operation for those who know little about it.'

During the production of the film Colonel John Waddy, who acted as one of the film unit's British technical advisers, and with whom I had served during the war, was reported as protesting about the inaccuracy of certain scenes; his advice was not taken, apparently.

For me, the film was like the curate's egg and therefore disappointing. The selection of the opening black and white original film shots of Eisenhower, Montgomery and Patton were surely not amongst the best of technical quality on record. The idea was good, but the shots failed to stress the intensity of the rancour between the latter two commanders and Eisenhower's unenviable task of keeping the balance.

Montgomery discredited, or ignored, intelligence reports that the 9th S.S. Panzer Division, and presumably the 10th and 11th were also in the Arnhem area, so anxious was he to prove his theory of the advantage of the single thrust, as well as ending the war by Christmas as he had predicted. This was the vital factor which gave the impetus to launch the operation regardless. Montgomery's determination in spite of intelligence reports led him to believe that merely by increasing the number of troops committed to the battle all opposition, known and unknown, would be overcome. The original plan was to use only the British 1st Parachute Brigade which was briefed for the operation a week before it actually took place. The troops were stood down and many went home on leave. A week later the British 1st Airborne Division and the Polish Parachute Brigade were briefed for the same operation. Men of the British 1st Parachute Brigade found it difficult to believe that the cancelled operation of a week ago was now to take place. They had been briefed for many operations which never took place, but never before for an operation that had been 'called off'. Now it was 'on' again, but this time with a very much larger force. It was not surprising therefore that some of the old sweats said, 'What the 'ell is goin' on?'

The sequences of the battle scenes were very difficult to follow, even with the aid of sub-titles and a knowledge of what actually happened.

The film also failed to explain how it was that John Frost and the 2nd Battalion reached the Arnhem road bridge with little opposition while the bulk of the remainder of the 1st Airborne Division was unable even to enter the town. No mention was made of the railway bridge which was destroyed and thus prevented the road bridge from being held by parachutists at both ends; had they been able to do so the battle of Arnhem might have been very different.

Understandably, a great part of the film was devoted to the gallant actions of the Americans at Grave and Nijmegen. The firm impression that I gained from the film was that the British 30 Corps, whose task it was to link up with the troops on the Arnhem bridge, was lethargic while the Americans were keen and eager to press on regardless. The only time during the performances (I saw the film four times) that I felt very close to reality were on those occasions when the Germans and the Dutch were on the screen.

I have no knowledge of the film industry and am therefore quite unable to judge whether *A Bridge Too Far* will be acclaimed in due course of time as a very good, bad or indifferent piece of entertainment; but it seemed to me that it was a film directed at being a financial bonanza rather than a film of history. No doubt I had a jaundiced view, and if I had, perhaps it was due to the advance publicity given to the cost of production, the very high fees paid to the leading actors of whom only Edward Fox (Lieut-General Brian Horrocks), Sir Laurence Olivier (Doctor Spaander) and Gene Hackman (Major-General Stanislaw Sosabowski) convinced me; Hardy Kruger made me feel that I was back in Oflag 79!

Whatever were the reasons for my disappointment, perhaps the spectacular confusion accompanied by an almost unceasing blast of pyrotechnics produced a nostalgia which inhibited my judgement.

Richard Spender wrote:

> One lonely, grim battalion cut its way
> Through agony and death to fame's high crown,
> And wonderingly watch the friendless strength
> Of little men, who die that the great Truths shall live.

I doubt if my experiences as a prisoner-of-war differed greatly from those of thousands of others, except for the fact that I was 'confined' for the relatively short period of eight months.

After surrender we were marched through the town with our hands above our heads. There were a number of Dutch civilians about and they stood still as we passed; their bewilderment was only equalled by our humiliation. Their former jubilation had vanished and no doubt they were considering the prospect of reprisals which might later be taken by the Germans, reprisals which, in fact, did follow.

As we passed through the main square no sound of a battle could be heard, neither from the outskirts of the town nor from the direction of the road bridge.

All pain and fatigue seemed to have vanished; my mind was filled with doubts and concern. We had killed a number of Germans, but had achieved little else unless we had kept them occupied during the vital period while John Frost and the 2nd Battalion were making their way to the bridge.

I could not be sure of the reaction of our captors since they were now fighting in their last ditch before the frontier of the 'Fatherland'. It occurred to me that once we had been screened we might be shot out of hand—it had been done before and prisoners at this stage of the war were an embarrassment as the frontiers closed in. Fortunately, my fears were without foundation, as time was to prove, but I was not to know this during those first few hours after capture.

The Germans who fought at the front were usually as considerate to their prisoners as we were to ours, but the further back you were taken into enemy territory so in proportion did the treatment change for the worse. Most fighting men have respect for each other when the fighting is done, but those in the rear echelons who are not involved in combat rarely have the understanding of those who have fought face to face and shared the same fears.

The men of 'C' Company in this small group marching through the town looked very tired, due in part to physical strain, but mainly I think because they shared my troubled mind. What would happen now? Was the battle for the bridge lost? Would there be an opportunity to escape? What news of the battle was reaching home? What was happening at the road bridge? As each question came unanswered so another took its place. Only one thing seemed certain—for us the war was over!

We reached a temporary P.O.W. collection area on the edge of

Arnhem where I was separated from my men. Exaggerated courtesy was shown to me by my escorts who took me to a large office within the main building.

In the room was an S.S. officer, two female typists and two German guards. I was invited to sit down, an invitation which I declined because my backside was still a bit sore. I was anxious—the attitude of my captors was much too reasonable to last. A cigarette was offered to me, which was declined. I lit one of my own. My batman, Private Kemsley, had produced a packet for me when we were separated. 'Free issue, sir, please take them,' he had said. He was a great chap—never forgot anything.

The preliminaries of the interrogation were unproductive, so the atmosphere changed quite suddenly. I was asked to undress in order that my clothing could be searched. The two female typists remained in the room while my clothes were removed—they giggled! I finally stood in my boots and socks and a field dressing round my buttocks, the latter failing to conceal that part of my anatomy which distinguished my sex. If the purpose was to anger, frighten or humiliate me—it failed. I only felt a growing surge of hate for these jack-booted Huns.

Eventually, I was allowed to dress. I felt pleased with myself because the search had proved abortive; they had failed to find a gold French 25 franc piece which was sewn into the lining of my beret, just behind the parachute badge. I still have that gold 25 franc piece. If it is War Department property, then they will have to come and find it, and I suspect that they would be no more successful than were those Germans.

I was marched away to a waiting vehicle—all the original courtesy had evaporated. I was to travel many miles before reaching my final abode, Oflag 79, Brunswick.

Unknown to me at this time, my father paid a visit to Grantham in the hope of gaining some first-hand information about the battle in general and me in particular. I had been reported officially 'missing' for the third time and he could not help but wonder if this time my luck had run out. He also wished to collect my personal belongings. It must have been a very sad shock to him when he discovered that all my kit, with a lot of others', had been stolen.

My escort in the vehicle—a rather large utility—were two soldiers who sat with me on the back seat, and a major who sat in the front with the driver. On our way we came across a bridge over a small river; the bridge was under repair—it had been bombed. The major seemed to be in a great hurry and ordered the driver to by-pass the barrier which had been set across the road, and in so doing the vehicle skidded down the bank and slid into the mud at the bottom. All my escort jumped out and started pulling and pushing to free the wheels which were deep in the mud. It was obvious that they would not be able to move it without a tow. So I remained where I was in the back seat. Eventually the vehicle was towed clear by a truck on the road. We continued our journey with my escort covered in mud from their boots to their waists—and their prisoner as dry as a bone! I laughed, the first time I had laughed for a long time! I don't think the major enjoyed the joke.

When we reached our destination, much to my surprise we were not at a military establishment, but in the beautiful garden of a Dutch house. There was a large lawn which covered most of the area and in the centre of the greensward were a garden table and several garden chairs. At the table was seated a rather insipid-looking German corporal with a file of papers in front of him. As my escort handed me over I believe the corporal asked why they were covered in mud and I was not. I also believe that the major gave him a pretty sharp reply. My new escort greeted me in perfect English and asked me to sit, which I did, very gently—the buggy ride had made my far end quite sore. The corporal spoke of the weather, which he suggested was very pleasant, the garden, the trees and the general surroundings—so reminiscent of England which was so near and yet, for me, so far away. He rambled on and asked me if I thought his English was good. When at last this obsequious corporal realized that I was very tired and in no mood for small-talk, he spoke in confidential terms and brought his chair closer as if not to be overheard. 'Now, Major, the intelligence officer will be here shortly, so let me see what I can do for you before he arrives. Would you like something to eat and would you like a wash?'

'Very much,' I replied.

'Very well. I will see the lady of the house and inquire if she will arrange.'

We went into the house where I met my hostess. She was Dutch and clearly moved by goodwill, whatever may have been her relations with the Germans. She spoke English quite well and was quick to tell me that she had visited London many times. She

113

invited me to the freedom of the bathroom and toilet. My thought that this might provide an opportunity to escape was quickly dispelled when the corporal insisted on keeping close attendance—waving his pistol.

Later we made our way back to the garden and the sunshine where I found that the table on the lawn had been laid. On the table was a tray on which were a cup of coffee, two fried eggs, some bread and an apple (apples again!) She had gone to a lot of trouble to show sympathy, or it might have been pity.

I expressed appreciation to this kind Dutchwoman, but I had no sooner picked up knife and fork when a German officer came from the house to join us.

He stormed across the lawn, strutted up to the table and peremptorily demanded what the food was doing on the table. The corporal was taken aback. He stood up, saluted and started to splutter an explanation all at one and the same time, but before he had time to get out more than a few words the officer snatched at the corner of the table and sent my tray of food and cup of coffee flying. In an almost hysterical voice he shouted at me in English, 'From now onwards you will be fed only by the German Reich!' I was then ordered into the house by this idiot who had robbed me of a good meal and had made a great mess on my hostess's lawn. The officer's English was nothing like as good as that of the corporal, but it was good enough to leave me in no doubt that he was not a man to be fooled with.

I was led into what must normally have been a small sitting-room which had now been converted into an office. There was a single bed against one of the walls. There were some dirty crocks on a small table and there was a smell of stale food. It appeared that this officer was billeted in the house and this room apparently was his bedroom, dining-room and office. There was a photograph on his desk which I assumed to be of his family—so he had some human instincts after all.

German interrogation did not lack either guile or thoroughness. It was not information of direct military significance which this officer sought—the purpose of the airborne operation 'Market Garden' must by then have been very clear. I had been in England only a few days before, while the majority of British troops captured had normally been in the line for weeks or months. Here was an opportunity to obtain up-to-date information on the effect of the V2; the extent of the bomb damage in the towns and ports; the morale of the civil population at home, and the current opinion in England as to the duration of the war. Whether or not this line of interrogation was for military purposes or for personal reassurance, I shall never know.

The conversation was one-sided so in the end I was given up as a bad job and escorted by my insipid corporal to a nearby guard-room. The Germans gave me the impression that they knew that they had lost the war, but were concerned about just when and how it would be lost. The Russians were advancing steadily on the eastern front!

On the following morning I was conveyed to the local station where I met several other prisoners. We were herded into a cattle truck (20 *hommes*—10 *chevaux*) and remained in it for the next few days. The travelling conditions were not good. Straw was on the floor of the truck and there were two metal buckets which danced about when the train was in motion—no matter when they were empty, but when they were full even 10 *chevaux* would have complained. My journey to Brunswick had started. It was to take me by way of Cologne and Coblenz, a journey down the Rhine, the beauty of which we were destined not to see.

After three days our train pulled into a small station 'somewhere in Germany'. It was afternoon. Our boots, which had been taken from us, were returned—there was some difficulty in sorting them out. The few Americans who were with us had the easiest job—their boots were brown! For the first time I was to hear the call, 'Alles aus, fünf!' which was the order to fall-in in five ranks. We were counted and marched off to another P.O.W. transit cage. Here we were fed with biscuits and dried sausage.

The weather was still fine and we sat in the sun and did our best to enjoy the rations which had been provided. It was then that about one hundred Flying Fortresses filled the sky. They flew over the top of the P.O.W. cage, jettisoning their bombs about a mile away. The vibrations were terrific. All the prisoners cheered. The guards were furious and fired shots into the air. We thought perhaps we had better stop cheering.

After the raid a dog-fight developed immediately overhead. Again cheers went up every time a fighter was shot down, although it was impossible to tell if they were Allies baling out or if they were Hun. More shots were fired into the air by the guards. This time they were a lot closer to the tops of our heads! Cheering ceased once more.

We had just been given the order to move again when an American pilot who had been shot down in the dog-fight was brought into the P.O.W. cage. Two hours before he had been in England—unbelievable! He distributed by far the greater part of his cigarettes to us—Americans are remarkably generous (how many remember the Marshall plan today, and how often has America been kicked in the teeth for her efforts?)

This pilot also produced a newspaper from his pocket. It had been published on that day. The headlines splashed the Arnhem battle in flaming banners. It was with mixed feelings that I read the report; there was no doubt that we had lost the battle and in so doing had paid a high price.

Our journey continued all that night. At each halt more prisoners joined the train and we were now a very mixed collection of nationalities; English, Scots, Americans, French, Canadians and Dutch; not all appeared to be official members of the forces of the countries of their origin. We made a further halt the following afternoon and this time we were taken to a *stalag* of Russian prisoners. There was a small wired enclosure into which we were marched. It was adjacent to the *stalag* and only a double wire fence separated us. The wire was some fifteen feet high with the usual sentry-boxes mounted high above the ground. The guards were numerous, which surprised me in view of the presumed state of German manpower; but most of the guards were old men.

We were each given some dried biscuits and a small tin of salt pork; the pork was almost all fat and therefore not easy to eat with enthusiasm. Having eaten more of this fat pork than was wise on pretty empty stomachs, a lot of us became sick later in the day—the buckets in the rail trucks became very full that night!

The Russians in the *stalag* seemed pleased to see us and sent up a great cheer as we entered our own wire cage. They were in a mood for fraternization and threw cigarettes to us over the intervening wire. The German guards disapproved and signalled to the Russians to withdraw from the wire. One Russian was a little slow in his retreat and one of the guards took deliberate aim and shot him. He did not move after he had fallen. At once another Russian ran from the large group to aid the man who had fallen. He was shot by the same guard before he was able to reach his comrade ... he did not move again. The echo of the shots could be heard in the silence. Two men died, shot out of hand, for no more than a contact with the outside world. When we were marched off to rejoin our train that evening, the bodies of the two Russians were still lying in the dust where they had fallen.

At home, the then British Foreign Secretary had agreed that the Russians were holding millions in concentration camps, including their own countrymen. One cannot always choose allies in times of war.

Our journey to Brunswick took us as far south as Coblenz where we had another halt. It was some time before the train could steam into the station due to an air raid on the town. We could hear the crump of the shells as they exploded; I am not sure if I ever came to terms with the pleasure of knowing that the Germans were taking a beating from these raids and the personal concern I had for my own safety while they lasted.

We were marched from the station through the town where the local population turned out to spit at us, not just one or two, but scores of them. I was grateful that the guards were with us, for if they had not been, I doubt if those Germans of Coblenz could have resisted violence. I suppose they had good reason to hate us.

Coblenz is a very attractive town, but we had little opportunity to see it. Having been herded from the train we were marched to a staging camp which provided a chance for our guards to get some rest and for the prisoners to have a wash and make use of reasonable latrines.

The camp was some two miles from the station and as we approached I could see the barbed wire fence and the wooden huts. I had worked my way to the rear of the column feigning a limp. It was my intention to make a dash for freedom should an opportunity arise. The opportunity came. The camp was some four hundred yards away and to my immediate right was a ditch at the side of the road. I decided that this was the moment.

The two guards on our flanks were just ahead of the rear of the column and there was no rear guard. I took my chance and jumped into the ditch. It was not very deep but sufficient to give me cover. I was grateful that it was dry although obviously part of a draining system. I was completely hidden from view and decided to wait for the column to move some way ahead before moving from my position. Just as I began to think that I had succeeded the column of prisoners was halted. There was a great deal of shouting by the guards and two of them suddenly ran back along the road looking into the ditch in which I was hiding. My fellow-prisoners began to sing, no doubt in order to create some confusion; those at the rear of the column had seen me make my leap.

I knew that I was in trouble and without weighing the possible cost I climbed out of the ditch and burst through the hedge into a field on the other side. The two guards saw me and followed in hot pursuit. It was hopeless, everywhere I looked there seemed to be obstacles, hedges, brick walls and buildings. I ran until I could run no more. My pursuers were rapidly catching up with me and, fearful that they might shoot, I stopped, turned and faced them. I cannot think why but I did not raise my hands in surrender, perhaps I was just too tired. The guards levelled their rifles at me as they approached and I thought to myself that my end was near. On reaching me they each took hold of one of my arms and almost gently returned me to the column. It seemed to me that I would be dealt with when we reached the staging camp. Nothing further happened. I shall never know nor understand why. Perhaps the guards were punished for allowing me to attempt to escape.

There was one other halt that I particularly remember. We had travelled north again and were forced to leave the train at the main station in Cologne because the railway line had been damaged in yet another air raid. We were hurriedly ushered on to the platform of the station from where we were led to an air raid shelter. I am not sure for whose safety this was, the guards' or ours. We remained in the shelter until dawn when we were taken back to our 'box cars'—the term used for our cattle trucks.

While on the station I could see the high structure of the cathedral. It looked like intricate black lace hung up against the pale morning sky. Smoke and fires surrounded the station—I recalled the smoke and fires on the road to Dunkirk.

At last we reached Brunswick and at last we would get some relief from the jolting 'box car'. During the day it became so hot in the confined space that sleep was almost impossible, and as the trains only moved at night, sleep was not easy. We were all very tired, filthy and hungry.

The reception always given to newly arrived 'kriegies' was warm. There was the renewed chance of getting up-to-date

Don't feel inferior to these new Airborne blokes

When airborne troops found themselves in Oflag 79, the old 'Kriegies' were much amused by the number of 'flashes' worn by the new arrivals. This cartoon was drawn by Frank Sharpley and published at various camps in Italy and Germany between 1942 and 1945. It was one of many which brilliantly portrayed life in 'the Bag'. The artist was an inmate of Oflag 79 and took the trouble after the war to ensure that his fellow prisoners-of-war did not forget the amusing side of their period in captivity.

119

information about the progress of the war and the possibility of further expertise being available from new talent—a wireless expert, perhaps, or even an experienced forger! The brilliance of the talent in a P.O.W. camp is an experience which I am glad to have had. If necessity is the mother of invention, then the mother of invention was herself a prisoner-of-war!

While I was in 'the Bag', I kept a diary provided by the War Prisoners' Aid of the Y.M.C.A., Geneva. Some of the notes I recorded in those days provide interesting reading today. For example, there is a recording of a 'short arm' inspection: 'It so happened that the Germans wished to make one of their numerous search inspections of the camp and its inmates. One of our number was advised that the medical inspections were thorough and that his rectum would come within the scope of the inspection. He therefore made preparations. The German medical officer carried out his duties with the usual scrupulous attention to detail. On examining this officer he discovered a piece of paper concealed in the aforementioned orifice. Taking great care in extracting his find he discovered the following inscription on the piece of paper, 'Heil Hitler! Look what I have found!'

There were other entries: '*March 28th.* 150 other ranks arrived in the camp today. They have been on the road walking for days. They are in a very bad way, dysentery, pneumonia, hunger and exposure. They have been moved away from the eastern front which must be pushing forward very quickly for the Hun to be moving P.O.W.s westwards. The Doc says they need urgent medical attention. Our rations for the next two days are to be given to them. This the Germans do not seem to understand.' Another entry records, 'A Russian told me today that it had been the practice in his camp to keep their dead for as long as possible. Conditions were so bad that they held their dead upright during roll calls in order to obtain a larger count and subsequently more rations. He is, I think, the only Russian in the camp.'

I only got into trouble once while I was in Oflag 79. I failed to salute the commandant and was duly charged. A few days later I was taken to the Commandant's office. I was marched in and my red beret was removed from my head with more than a little force. I was told to salute. I refused, explaining that British officers did not, unlike the Americans, salute with their hats off. An argument followed. I think I won the argument because I never did salute the

Commandant, but I paid for my victory by being given 7 days in solitary confinement.

It was very difficult to escape from Oflag 79, and for a number of reasons. The wire was so far away from most of the houses in which we lived as to make tunnelling almost impossible. The area surrounding the camp was exposed, dogs and guards were numerous. There was, however, an escape which is worth recording because of its simplicity and because it illuminated a very difficult decision which P.O.W.s had to make during the last stages of the war.

Those who know of the escapes from Colditz will appreciate that the German security at Oflag 79 was nothing like as sophisticated as at that establishment, neither was the camp such a great physical obstacle. However, a very efficient and active escape committee existed. The war was obviously coming to an end and it is not surprising, therefore, that there was more than one opinion with regard to escaping at this time. It was not known what action the Germans would take when the Allies were nearing the gates of the camp; it was speculated by some that there was an even chance that all prisoners would be shot. This was not beyond the bounds of possibility. The word of the Führer was still sacred in Germany—and was he not a madman? All agreed in principle that it was the duty of every prisoner to attempt to escape, but a factor now to be taken into consideration was the possibility of reprisals on those left behind. This was particularly relevant since the Germans were getting more jumpy as each day passed. Had they not issued an order stating, 'It is no longer a sport for prisoners to attempt to escape. Those who are caught will be shot.' It was a difficult decision in the circumstances prevailing at that time; I am still uncertain of the answer. Many prisoners had been in captivity for four years and were in no physical condition to make an attempt.

However, an escape was made. A number of German workmen were in the camp carrying out essential sanitary repairs. It was decided that these workmen provided an opportunity for one or two, not more, to leave the hospitality of the Third Reich. The workmen left the camp at odd times during the day in order to fetch further materials. If a P.O.W. dressed up as one of these workmen there was a chance that he could bluff his way through the main gate. All he would have to do would be to approach the sentry and say, 'aus', and then walk out. As simple as that!

Assuming that the sentry was caught off guard, there were still two major problems: the attention of the guard had to be drawn away from his duty, so someone would offer him cigarettes in exchange for some useless information. There were plenty of officers in the camp who could speak fluent German. The guards were always glad to get cigarettes—who was not! The second problem was to get past the guard-room without being seen and then pass through the second gate, which was also guarded by a sentry. It so happened that there was a latrine behind the guard-room; once the escaper had passed through the first gate he could make straight for this latrine. Here he would go through the motions of relieving himself and when he had finished he would return to the road leading to the second gate by passing round the far side of the guard-room and thus avoid exposing himself to view from the guard-room window. He would then proceed to the second gate and request that the sentry open it with the single magic word, 'aus'. With a bit of luck this sentry would assume that all was well, since there had been no challenge at the first gate. It would then only remain for the escaper to walk slowly round the camp (under the eyes of the guards in the watch-towers) and make his way into the woods. Here he could change into French working clothes carried in a sack over his shoulder and pass as a French worker deported from France. All clothes and papers would be provided by the experts of the escape committee—money, *Ausweis*, maps, possible contacts, food and so on.

So it was planned—and so it was carried out—and it worked!

Two prisoners escaped by this method and without a hitch. However, a third was caught because he overdid his disguise—he carried a broken lavatory seat over his arm. All went well until he reached his routine at the rear of the guard-room; it was here that he encountered a German officer also relieving himself. While so doing the officer asked the would-be escaper why he was carrying the lavatory seat. There was no answer; there could not be, because the prisoner could speak no German.

The escapes were loyally covered for several days by those left at the camp. Stand-in arrangements were made during roll-calls until it was assumed that sufficient time had elapsed to allow the escapers to get well away from the camp area. When at last the

Germans were told of the escape there followed a good deal of shouting and a thorough roll-call.

It was important for the camp commandant to discover just how many of his charges were missing. Each hut in which we were housed was searched and while these searches were in progress we were lined up and checked, one by one, by being called out by name and identified with a photograph on our record papers. The check proved to be a fiasco because every time the Germans called out an English name in a guttural voice we would mimic the sound loudly by calling the German pronunciation. More often than not it was impossible to recognize the name being called, for example, when the name 'Marcperesoorn' was called and repeated by the P.O.W.s in loud voices, poor MacPherson standing at the back of the line had not the faintest idea that it was his name that was being called. This procedure continued until the Germans gave up in despair.

In 'the Bag' I met Bill Bowes, the Yorkshire fast bowler and a schoolboy hero of mine; Freddie Brown, one-time captain of England; 'Pip' Gardener, V.C., and many others who made my brief stay behind barbed wire seem a great deal shorter than it was. So much talent in such a confined space! Gordon Horner produced a brilliant book of drawings which he called *For You The War is Over*, which portrays more accurately the life of a prisoner-of-war than any written word could possibly achieve.

The inmates of Oflag 79 were freed in May 1945 by the Americans. We remained in the camp for three days following our freedom. They were three very uncomfortable days because for the first time for many months there was as much food available as we could eat. The result was that food and wine played havoc with shrunken stomachs and it was necessary to construct a large number of emergency latrines in order to accommodate two thousand 'Kriegies' who wanted to go to the toilet at one and the same time!

Five days after release I was back in England, having spent one night in Brussels. Doug Crawley and I had shared the same room in the P.O.W. camp and he accompanied me on the night out in Brussels, but our hearts were not in the bright lights—we just wanted to get home.

My arrival in north London was not the happiest of returns. I found that my parents' house had been hit by a bomb and close friends of the family had been killed. My mother had been unhurt, but my father had suffered a very serious injury. I think I felt a stronger hate for the Hun then than at any other during the war.

My normal weight was eleven and a half stone, but after only a few months in 'the Bag' it had been reduced to eight stone. However, the family had stockpiled its rations for my return and it did not take long before I was back to my normal weight.

In after-years, it is difficult to recapture experiences in perspective. The Germans were past-masters in the process of proving themselves justified in their actions. The subsequent history of Russian aggression and penetration has played into the hands of German apologists. The human mind has an extra-ordinary capacity for discarding from memory that which it desires to forget. This process cannot justify, for example, the fact that the Nazi régime did enter into an unholy alliance with Russia before they undertook the rape of Poland. No doubt, had the Germans been the victors of the Second World War, they would themselves have attempted to subjugate Russia and thus might have halted the spread of Communism, at least for a generation. Their triumph, however, would certainly have imposed on the world for years a totalitarian form of rule which, in its denial of individual liberty, might have been indistinguishable from a threat which we still may have to face. Of two such great evils, can one be considered less than the other?

One morning, after I had been home on leave for about three weeks, a telegram arrived for me from Brigadier Gerald Lathbury. It was to the point: 'Will you command parachute company 8th Battalion, 6th Airborne Division, destined service in the Far East? I joined the 8th Battalion within 48 hours; it was under the command of Lieut.-Colonel George Hewetson, D.S.O., O.B.E. (who was often heard to say, 'I am the strongest living man I know!') However, within weeks, instead of the Far East, I found myself serving in Palestine under that very likeable commander. Now both Germany and Japan had surrendered.

*Jaffa Arab*

# 5

# *The Not So Holy Land*

The War in Europe had ended with the unconditional surrender of Germany. Russia had raced forward to Berlin and the Allies were left with unsatisfactory lines of demarcation—the 'cold war' in luke-warm form had already begun.

The Marshall Plan, which provided for the economic recovery of the 'free' world, including Germany and, later Japan, was in its early stages. It was a plan which was never fully appreciated by those who benefited from it. The United States was yet to learn the price that invariably has to be paid in cash, conscience and lives for being a philanthropic world power. This mighty and generous nation found itself, for the first time, involved in world leadership.

One of the immediate concerns following the war was the problem of establishing a Jewish state in Palestine against a background of Arab hostility. Great Britain was enmeshed in the Jewish–Arab problem, mainly resulting from the terms of the Balfour Declaration which promised a permanent home for the Jews in Palestine. Jewish immigrants from Europe, following the end of hostilities, poured into this narrow strip of land at the eastern end of the Mediterranean. British troops were sent to the area in order to restrict the great influx of Jewish immigrants and, at the same time, to try to reduce the tension between Arab and Jew.

It was in these circumstances that the 3rd Parachute Brigade, of which the 8th Battalion was a part, was sent to Palestine in the autumn of 1945, for the purpose of giving 'aid to the civil power', instead of to the Far East, which was the original intention.

The *Manual of Military Law* on the subject of 'aid to the civil power', specifically laid down the principles to be observed, as follows:

'When called to the aid of the civil power, soldiers in no way differ in the eyes of the law from other citizens, although, by reason of their organization and equipment, there is always a danger that their employment in aid of the civil power may in itself constitute more force than is necessary.

The law is clear that a soldier must come to the assistance of the civil authority where it is necessary for him to do so, but not otherwise. No excess of force or display must be used, and a soldier is guilty of an offence if he uses that excess, even under the direction of the civil authority, provided he has no such excuse as that he is bound in the particular circumstances of the case to take the facts, as distinguished from law, from the civil authority.

Though there is no legal difference between soldiers and other citizens in respect to the duty to respond to the call of the civil authority, there is, in cases of disturbance where the civil authority has not asked for help, a duty to take action laid upon military commanders which is not laid upon other citizens, except magistrates and peace officers, and even though the civil authority should give directions to the contrary, the commander of the troops, if it is really necessary, is bound to take such action as the circumstances demand.'

It has been commented that the whole quotation provided a most convenient umbrella for the politician and for the civil power, leaving the military holding the baby. If anything went wrong the military could be held to blame, for using either too much or too little force, or for not taking action or, alternatively, using no force when it should have done so. After the event, anyone who wished could produce adequate reasons for placing the blame on the military. The burden of decision was always on the soldier, and I am not sure that even today the weight of that burden has shifted.

British troops in Palestine at this time suffered the same kind of indignities, frustrations and casualties which they were to experience later in Northern Ireland. Terrorist tactics do not change: riots and destruction, mass assaults with women and children to the fore, indiscriminate use of explosives, kidnapping, ambush killings and atrocities to frighten the local population and to frustrate security forces, both military and police. Palestine was an unhappy country. A thriving oasis of industry and success in the middle of a sand-swept wilderness was in itself a constant source of envy to the surrounding Arab nations. If there were no oil in the Middle East one is bound to wonder how the Arabs would survive, certainly not on the fish from the Sweet Water Canal in Egypt, which is surely the most stinking strip of water in the world.

The Airborne troops in this theatre of operations played their role with restraint in spite of great provocation; the Stern Gang, I.Z.L. and Hagannah knew all there was to know of terrorism, learned, I suspect, in part from experiences in Germany.

Neither Jew nor Arab accepted the presence of the British Army in Palestine. The former because the troops harassed the landings of Jewish immigrants, that is, those who attempted to enter the country in excess of the British Government quota. The terrorist activities of the Jews (they saw them as liberation activities) were concentrated against the British soldier who was attempting, peacefully, to do his job. That was a period of Jewish history of which they cannot be proud. One of the principal leaders of the Jewish terrorist organization at that time, Begin, is now the Prime Minister of Israel.

The Arabs found it impossible to accept the Balfour Declaration and therefore could not accept its perpetrators.

A number of experiences—of varying kinds—came my way whilst serving with the 8th Battalion in that country which is now Israel. I was fortunate enough to meet an adventurous Royal Engineer, Major John Cowtan, M.C., who persuaded me to go on a shooting trip to Lake Hula to the north of Lake Tiberius. The duck were reputed to fly over the lake in such numbers as to blot out the rising sun; all day they would sit on the lake and at night fly off again, and so thick was the flight at night that the sun seemed to set an hour earlier!

It was a memorable shooting trip. We spent one evening at the Tiberius Hotel beside the lake. Before dawn we made our way to Lake Hula. Hired boat-hands quietly rowed us towards the reeds at the northern end of the lake. As the sun rose so did the ducks—hundreds and hundreds of them. I was never a good shot, ——but I could not miss bagging twenty brace in as many minutes. We returned to the Tiberius Hotel well pleased with ourselves. My ducks were tied up by their feet and hung in my jeep on the crossbars which supported the tarpaulin cover behind the driver's seat.

The following morning, Sunday, we were due to return to the Battalion based a few miles south of Tel Aviv. My driver arrived at 9 a.m. and by the look on his face I could see that there was trouble. He told me that all the duck had been eaten, by what he did not know. The vehicle was covered in blood and feathers. On examination, my worst fears were confirmed. Only one edible duck remained—all the rest had been devoured during the night by some wild beast, or, more likely, by local dogs.

When I returned to the Battalion I was told that either I had not been on a shooting trip or, obviously, I needed to go on a small arms course. Who could possibly return from a shoot on Lake Hula with only one duck? From that day I was frequently referred to as 'Wahid Bat Dover', which, I believe, freely translated from the Arabic, means 'One-Duck Dover'.

It was my association with John Cowtan which gave me an experience which I shall ever remember with wonder and satisfaction. John planned a trip to Petra—the 'rose-red city half as old as time'. The expedition was arranged. We took three jeeps, each with a trailer loaded with food, water (and some stronger liquid), petrol and oil. Our route from Tel Aviv took us north to Damascus and then south to Amman, Petra and Akaba. It was planned to return to Tel Aviv from Akaba by way of the Wadi Akaba and Beersheba—a round trip of about a thousand miles.

The drive to Damascus presented no problem since the third-class road across the plateau left one no chance to lose one's way. However, the journey was not without surprise—we drove through a snow blizzard which swept across the plateau and the temperature dropped below zero.

Damascus was a fascinating place. The inhabitants were at that time pro-British, but the French were not in favour. In the bazaar the craftsmen were fabricating all the wares for which Damascus is famous: brasswork of great beauty, brocades in gold and silver, mosaic woodwork, and the rest—all very intriguing and everything done by hand in the most primitive fashion. We visited the 'Street called Straight', but the women for sale or hire were pathetically unattractive.

We travelled south from Damascus and stayed the night in a

desert fort with the Arab Legion. We heard first-hand stories of Lawrence of Arabia and learned to drink thick Arabic black coffee well into the night.

We pushed on to Amman and continued south to Petra, but now there was no road and direction was kept by compass. What an amazing part of the world—miles and miles of sand, not a tree, not a feature—just sand, and more sand. The jeeps, so far, had behaved very well and were not overheating, but I began to wonder what we would do should there be a breakdown. We were miles from anywhere—I visualized a Court of Inquiry as to why two officers used W.D. transport to go on a tour of Arabia.

At last we came to Petra. What an astonishing sight it was—a city carved out of the solid rock in the crater of an extinct volcano. To reach that ancient city we had to make our approach on foot leaving our vehicles behind under guard of one of our drivers.

The classical name Petra, and the early name Sela, have the same meaning; 'Rock'. It is not difficult to understand why Petra was given such a name in view of the wild and fantastic shapes of the hills and chasms which surround it. The entrance itself is by way of a very narrow crevice in the rock, called the Siq, the sides of which are so high and overhanging that from time to time the sky is blotted out. After stumbling over the rough ground for half a mile we reached the sight that is impossible to describe; the sudden change from the gloom of the Siq hurt the eyes and gradually one's consciousness absorbed the flaming beauty and perfect proportions of the great tomb of Khazneh—the old Treasury. The urn which has been carved at the summit bears the marks of many bullets which have been fired in the hope of shattering it in order to release its legendary treasure.

How strange it was to find this ancient monument to civilization in the middle of the desert. Many of the tombs were occupied by Arabs and after dark their fires made tiny points of light in the darkness. The whole place had a mystic kind of magic.

Little is known of the city's early history and the first reliable mention dates back to 312 B.C. when Petra was captured by Antigonus. He was perhaps the founder of Petra as a haven for thieves who extracted toll from the caravans crossing the desert.

From the nearby Wadi Musa a channel was cut in the rock to the heart of Petra in order to produce a continuous supply of fresh water. From time to time the water was cut off and Petra was put to siege. To overcome this, great reservoirs were hewn in the rock to collect the rainwater as it poured into little channels which led to the reservoirs.

In 1946, when I visited Petra, birds and beasts of prey hunted through the once busy streets of this ancient city, the water channels had silted up and nature was continuing its process of inexorably eradicating the works of man.

I was very sorry to leave this fascinating place because there was so much to explore, but our leave was limited and we still had a long way to go. However, there was a slight delay before we could continue our journey south to Akaba. A bent axle was the result of hitting a rock during our approach to Petra and it was impossible for the vehicle to continue without some repairs. We were no blacksmiths, but with the aid of the enthusiasm of a number of young Arabs and a Heath Robinson set of bellows, we managed to repair the damage; at least, the wheels now rotated without screeching to high heaven.

The hospitality extended to us by the Arab Legion continued as we made our way south —this was indeed the country of Lawrence of Arabia and we were told many stories of his exploits by our hosts. The torture of drinking Arab coffee into the early hours, squatting on the floor and not daring to ask to be excused in spite of bursting internal pressures, was the price we had to pay for our overnight stay at each Arab fortress. I have often wondered why our Arab hosts managed to sit for so long without apparent discomfort. Perhaps they had learned something from their camels!

When we reached Akaba I was disappointed—perhaps Petra was still very much in my mind. There was nothing at Akaba except a deep-freezing plant for the red mullet which the Arab fishermen took from the Red Sea. We only stayed for one night, but this gave us an opportunity to have a bathe in the sea—the first 'bath' we had had for ten days.

The return trip to Tel Aviv, by way of Beersheba, continued to present surprises. Gazelle running wild were beautiful to see—a pity, but we had to shoot one for food. The crimson, blue and red mountains which skirted the Wadi Akaba seemed to enclose the desert as the sides of a furnace. The sand was so hot that it was not possible to put a naked foot to the ground. The Wadi Akaba, as magnificent as it is, can be merciless to those without water or wagon.

On our arrival back at camp we came sharply back to reality. Our leave was over and the purpose of our being in Palestine was instantly apparent. The Jews had blown up a number of aircraft on Lydda airfield; three paratroops had been garroted in an orange grove by the I.Z.L.; four guards had been shot and the King David Hotel in Jerusalem had suffered severe damage from a bomb explosion. Everyone was too busy to listen to the stories of our journey through Jordan. Indeed, we found so much to do on our return that there was no time to relate them. This was just as well in view of the fact that my damaged jeep had developed a serious grinding noise in its front axle and I hoped that the flurry of activity would divert those who might otherwise ask embarrassing questions.

There were two diversions from routine patrols, cordons and searches: my old 2nd Battalion of the Parachute Regiment had arrived in Palestine and this gave me an opportunity to meet old friends, including Doug Crawley and Duncan McLean; more important, however, was a decision to 'show the flag' at Khartoum in the Sudan.

On 6 May 1946, a composite group of parachutists under the command of Lieut.-Colonel George Hewetson, D.S.O., O.B.E., was ordered to make a parachute descent on the aerodrome at Khartoum, where the Blue Nile and the White Nile meet. I was to command a company of the group. The opportunity to visit the Sudan does not often present itself. It is a country which in the latter half of the last century saw a feat of arms as glorious as any in which the British Army has taken part.

We flew from Palestine to Wadi Halfa, about five hundred miles south of Cairo, and after a night's rest flew on the next morning to Khartoum. When the aircraft arrived over the dropping-zone—Khartoum aerodrome—a combination of rising hot air and a very high wind, of almost gale force, created the elements of disaster. As the men jumped out of the aircraft and their parachutes developed they were either swept upwards by hot air currents, instead of descending, or slipped through the air streams and were dragged along the ground at great speed by the wind without being able to collapse their parachutes. Out of the total force of some 143 men, 97 suffered injuries, 34 of whom were admitted to hospital, and 4 lost their lives.

The drop should never have been made. Once parachutists have been committed to the air nothing can be done to pull them back into the aircraft. If, because of a strong wind, a man is unable to collapse his parachute upon landing, he will be dragged along the ground at the speed of the wind. If he is lucky he will be on his back which will enable him to dig his heels into the ground and pull on his liftwebs, but if he is face down to the ground his elbows and knees invariably take the drag.

At Khartoum, the men were dragged along the hard surface of the aerodrome runway until their 'chutes collapsed on being blown against one of the buildings on the edge of the airfield, or, in some cases, until jeeps were motored into the 'chutes for the specific purpose of collapsing them. Many knees and elbows were skinned to the bone, a number of men concussed and much equipment damaged.

The 'flag' was certainly put on display, but just what the inhabitants of Khartoum made of it is difficult to assess. The responsibility of a dropping-zone safety officer is very great: it is he who fires the green Very light to let the aircraft pilots know that ground and air conditions are favourable for jumping. His task is never made easier if the political stakes are high and senior officers are expecting 'a good show'.

When I left my aircraft I found it difficult to believe that I was not still attached to the fuselage, because the ground below me appeared to be moving so very fast. On looking up I could see that my parachute was fully developed; it was not, as normal, somewhere above my head, but level with my shoulders and remaining steady. I was being swept along almost parallel to the ground at great speed. Seconds passed, and as I held tightly to my liftwebs it became clear that I was not descending. The aerodrome disappeared and I found myself drifting at a great rate over the town heading towards a railway line and some high-tension cables. There was nothing that I could do: to 'milk' my 'chute might cause it to collapse. My flight through the air suddenly terminated as my body crashed against a pylon and my 'chute burst into flames on contact with the high-tension cables. I remembered no more—except the sensation of falling.

I woke up in Khartoum Hospital and felt almost as sore as I had been on the lava slopes of Mount Etna, but there was something different. My left thigh was very swollen and my old wound had split open, and the right side of my body was blistered and sunburned. This I could not understand until the Sister in charge of the ward explained to me that when brought to the hospital I was both unconscious and naked. I had been found without boots, socks, vest or equipment; indeed, I was as naked as when I was born, and almost as messy. It seemed that some Sudanese had found me and taken me for dead and—as is the custom in that part of the world—findings is keepings! They had stripped me of literally everything I possessed!

After a few days I was transported back to Sarafand Hospital in Palestine and it was while in hospital that I learned that I had been selected to lead the Airborne jeep column in the Victory Parade in London. The prospect of leave and a return to England was a far better tonic than any doctor could have prescribed.

My leave in England was memorable for a number of reasons. I visited the families of the men who had lost their lives on the jump at Khartoum. All the men of the Company had forfeited one week's pay and this substantial sum of money was put in my care to distribute to the families which I considered to be most in need. The largest donation went to a pretty young wife, now a widow, who had both legs in irons. Her young son, aged three, was already the image of his father, whom he would never see again. What a disgrace it is that the next of kin of servicemen, men killed in the course of their duties, have to be given financial aid in this way or through regimental associations. Life, as untimely death, is ever unjust.

The experience of participating in the Victory Parade was great fun, but I wondered if the expense was justified. While sitting in my jeep very early in the morning of the day of the Parade, I noticed Field Marshal Alexander walking by himself past my column. I jumped out of the jeep and approached him and asked if I could be of any assistance. He seemed to be lost, but in reply to my inquiry he said, 'No, I'm not lost and I need no help, but thank you. I am enjoying some early morning fresh air and nostalgia.'

In my view, 'Alex' was the greatest soldier of the Second World War.

It was while living under canvas in Regent's Park prior to the Parade that I backed Airborne to win the Derby. This splendid grey colt passed the post ahead of the field at odds of 66-1. Mr Leonard Gullick, the host of the 19th Club in Old Burlington

Street, placed the bet for me, and paid up promptly! Having placed five pounds on this horse I did very well and I had a very good leave.

This leave differed from all others, not because I became engaged—since I had succumbed to that point of courtship with other young ladies on five previous occasions—but because this time I not only became engaged, I also got married. My method of proposal was perhaps a little unusual. I had known the lady since she was fourteen years of age and she knew of my previous escapades and therefore I had grave doubts as to whether my proposal would be accepted. So, I decided to write a letter to her father and to ask for his blessing. The posting of the letter was so timed that it would be received after the lady in question had left her home to visit me. On her arrival I showed her the letter which I had written to her father and waited for the response. My wife-to-be was so taken aback that, at first, I thought I was to be rejected. However, to my everlasting good fortune and gratitude she accepted and we were married within a month. After a brief honeymoon of only four days, I was recalled to Palestine. The Battalion could not possibly know that I was on my honeymoon, and even if they had I very much doubt if it would have made the slightest difference to my recall.

By this time, airborne units were in a state of flux since most of the experienced officers had more than completed their term with the airborne arm. A number were being posted to staff appointments, or were returning to their own regiments. Arriving back with the 8th Battalion I learned that there was an anticipated move to Germany and at that time I had no wish to serve in that country. I had been away from my mother Regiment—the Queen's Own Royal West Kent Regiment—for a very long time. So, after attending the Staff College at Haifa I rejoined the 1st Battalion of the Queen's Own stationed at Suez.

I had last been with this Battalion at Dunkirk and it felt strange to return and no longer wear a red beret. None the less, it was good to be back and to meet old friends again, but it was noticeable how few of the 'originals' had survived the years of war.

My last memory on leaving Palestine was a sad one. In the early days of the riots in Tel Aviv I found a truly magnificent alsatian dog lying in the gutter of one of the streets. His left front paw was bleeding and the centre pad of this foot had been eaten away. He was friendly when I approached him and made not the slightest fuss when I lifted him up and put him in my jeep. I took him back to camp with me and decided to keep him and call him Genghis Khan, because he was so fearsome and strong. The paw was badly infected and he was unable to put it to the ground. My batman, Private William Beebe (later to be a police constable in Peterborough), became as fond of Khan as I did and we both nursed him until his foot was healed. A boot was made for his paw; it had a centre support which took the place of the missing pad which made it possible for him to walk and run with only the slightest limp. Khan was my constant companion and we became great friends. What fools men are about their dogs, especially if they are soldiers!

I had to leave Khan in Palestine when I returned to England for the Victory Parade. On my return I was shocked to see that his paw had deteriorated to such an extent that the local vet advised amputation as high as the knee. Beebe was very worried, but he had no need to be because the condition of Khan's paw was not due to lack of attention. I just could not face the prospect of this magnificent beast hobbling about on three and a half legs, so I made the decision—Khan was shot. William Beebe volunteered to do the task for me in spite of the fact that he was almost as upset as I was. I buried Khan in the sands of Sarafand.

Leaving Airborne and returning to my Regiment in Egypt was a traumatic change, not just the return of a prodigal son—I missed Genghis Khan.

I passed through Cairo on my way to Suez and noticed that many German prisoners of war were still employed as orderlies in the transit camp. Their arrogance had completely vanished and in its place was a nauseating obsequiousness, but they had not forgotten how to work hard.

Cairo was back to normal and the bars were flourishing. Thieves were on the rampage in the streets and dirty picture postcards were for sale at every corner. Pornography was rife in Egypt long before it became a lucrative business in Europe. Indeed, Egypt boasted a museum of pornography which I saw, and this apart from the private collection of King Farouk which, of course, I never saw!

By contrast, Suez was a dreary town and not enhanced by the military camps which comprised tents pitched in rows behind barbed wire. The troops were bored and training was restricted to firing on the range and undergoing camp guard duties. There were no amusements outside the camp area and short leaves in Port Said and Cairo were expensive.

Mercifully, I only spent five months in Suez, during which time two recollections remain very clear. Major Derek Scull, an old friend and fellow officer of the Regiment, was invited to participate in a bridge drive to be held at the only decent club in Suez—the French Club. He asked me to join him as his partner. My standard of play was high at that time since I had had plenty of practice whilst in 'the Bag'. Derek's standard was very high. On the appointed Wednesday evening we were welcomed warmly by the members of the club, and after the drive were equally warmly applauded for gaining the highest score and taking first prize. We were invited again the following week, but on winning the first prize again we were not so warmly applauded. On our third visit, the combination of steady play and very good cards gave us first prize for the third time. The applause when we received our prize on this occasion was very faint—and we were never invited again! Perhaps they thought that we were cheating, but in fact we both held cards of such strength during the whole period that a novice could not have failed to make continuous contracts.

At this time Field Marshal Montgomery decided to tour the Middle East and address as many officers as he could who were stationed in that area. Great security precautions were taken to ensure that there would be no danger of about a thousand officers being blown up while he talked to them in a large hall at Ismailia.

I was never quite sure of the purpose of this address, but it left me in no doubt that this 'Little Caesar' was determined that no one should forget him, particularly as he was now a Field Marshal. We had all been briefed that there was to be no smoking and no coughing while he spoke. He arrived a few minutes late, but I fancy this was deliberate. Monty was a master at stage management and always ensured that an atmosphere of great moment was created even if it didn't exist before his arrival.

I came away from that 'pep talk' full of admiration. He gave a marvellous performance in telling us how he had won the war and would shortly win the peace. None the less, the feeling I had experienced when he first addressed the 1st Parachute Brigade in North Africa returned. He was magnificent, but seemed to fail to have the genuine common touch. I am quite sure that I would not have enjoyed being a member of his personal staff. Francis de Guingand, who had been his Chief of Staff, must have been a remarkable man to have served Monty so well and for so long and one is left wondering how much of Monty's glory was due to this brilliant staff officer.

Good fortune was smiling on me. There was a vacancy which had to be filled on a company commander's course in England and it was suggested that I might like to fill it. An opportunity to rejoin my wife, whom I had left in London immediately after our honeymoon, and the chance to get out of the environment of Suez was not to be missed. I was duly sent on the course.

Just before I left an amusing incident occurred. The Battalion rifle team competed in a firing competition between a number of regiments and King Farouk's personal bodyguard. The King himself had arranged the match and was to present a handsome cup to the winning team. My Regimental team had practised hard—since they had little else to do—and in consequence had become very good. It did not surprise me that the team won the competition. However, it surprised King Farouk. To put it mildly, he was furious that the team from his personal bodyguard had been defeated. As he was about to present the cup it fell to the floor. Some said he threw it!

After a few days' leave in London I reported to the School of Infantry at Warminster. On arrival at this very efficient establishment my conscience pricked me: I admitted to myself that the eagerness with which I had accepted the vacancy was entirely due to my desire to leave Suez—I had no enthusiasm for standing out in the rain and answering questions based on tactical exercises without troops!

A night exercise had been arranged whereby small groups were required to find their way in the dark to an objective by means of a number of different compass bearings. I was put in charge of one group, and it occurred to me that it was pretty pointless to march for many miles on different compass bearings when, by tracing the given bearings on a map, a straight line could be drawn from the starting-point to the objective. It would be a simple matter then to march along that straight line and, of course, the distance would be much shorter. So, that is what my group did—and with unfortunate results.

The object turned out to be a tank in the middle of a field. We reached it, not surprisingly, much earlier than had been anticipated by the directing staff, with the result that they were caught unawares. I gave my little group orders to attack. We threw thunder-flashes and fired Very lights—in consequence the whole area was lit up like a summer sunset. The shouts of fury from the directing staff could surely have been heard miles away. We had wrecked the whole exercise since all the other groups had no difficulty in seeing exactly where the objective was. Initiative, sometimes, can be carried too far!

I know that I was not the only one who found it difficult to 'play' at soldiers immediately following the war. It was not so much that one felt that the courses were a waste of time, but rather that they made a mockery of recent experiences which had been very unpleasant.

My report from the course was probably not as bad as it should have been. In any case, I was not returned to the Regiment, I was posted to the staff of Eastern Command at Hounslow, where I met for the first time General Sir Gerald Templer—a real professional if ever there was one—and under whose command I was to serve again later in Malaya. I enjoyed this, my first staff appointment, because it gave me many opportunities to play cricket.

Then followed a period which I spent under the trees at Wilton Park, Beaconsfield, which was the home of the School of Military Administration. If environment has any part of inspiration, then Wilton Park was an ideal place for such a military school. As I have said earlier, there is no better way to learn than to be an instructor, and at the School of Military Administration I learned a great deal about accountancy, records, pay and military law. My period as an instructor also brought home the fact that peacetime administration was a very different thing from administration in war—the words 'write-off' were replaced in peacetime by 'Courts of Inquiry' and 'Courts Martial'. No longer could mishaps be brushed aside: an officer would invariably be invited to pay, or, as an alternative, resign his commission! This was an important period for the Army: we all had to learn over again that stores and equipment were not expendable as in war and that almost limitless funds were no longer available. As Kipling wrote, 'For it's Tommy this, an' Tommy that, an' Tommy, wait outside' but it's 'Special train for Atkins when the trooper's on the tide.' The tide had gone out!

It was at Wilton Park that I met Ronnie Rutter, six feet seven inches tall, and surely as fast a bowler as ever seen in amateur cricket. When playing for the Minor Counties against the Australians he had taken the wickets of Bradman, Ponsford and McCabe, proof of which could be seen in the photographs which lined the staircase in his house. In each instance the three stumps were shattered.

I had many enjoyable games of cricket on the Beaconsfield ground and had the distinction of being bowled out by Sir Leary Constantine and by the son of R. W. V. Robins who was then a pupil at Eton College. I also had the pleasure of hitting one six out of the ground, over the road and into the garden of Parkside, where we rented the ground floor of that beautiful house. The ball was never found and I was glad that I was not asked to pay for its replacement! The locals pulled my leg and said that it went through the upstairs window of a bus and travelled to Piccadilly. This was, of course, nonsense, because buses from Beaconsfield did not go to Piccadilly.

By the end of 1950 I was called to rejoin my Regiment, which was about to embark for service in Malaya.

*Eastern Intellect ...*

# 6

# Terrorism in Malaya

When the Japanese capitulated and their troops were withdrawn from Malaya at the end of the war, a large number of Communists and underground guerrillas who had been fighting against the Japanese occupation forces remained in the jungle (*ulu*). They retained their arms and continued their terrorist activities, but their fight was now against what they termed 'the Imperialist British occupation of Malaya'.

These Communist guerrillas were supported and inspired by both Russia and China and they formed part of the Communist expansion plan to infiltrate the 'soft' areas exposed immediately following the end of the war. The Malayan Communist Party had failed to infiltrate the various trade unions in sufficient strength to gain control; this was mainly due to the multi-racial population comprising Malays, Chinese, Indians and Tamils.

The Communist Terrorists (C.T.s) were not a rabble, they were highly organized, uniformed, well equipped with weapons, an efficient communications system to the Political Commissars, and above all they were fanatics in the extreme. The forces of the C.T.s were divided into three main groups: firstly, the jungle soldier; secondly, the Min Yuen—also operating from the jungle, but in plain clothes; and, finally, the terrorist 'killer squads' which were used for the purpose of intimidation, extortion and murder of the vilest kind. This last group had the specific duty of murdering selected people, such as vigilant white planters, unco-operative heads of the labour forces on the rubber and palm oil estates, and high personages.

It was a thoroughly unpleasant situation and the jungle provided

143

perfect cover from which the C.T.s were able to operate. I have never understood why Spencer Chapman, with all his experience, considered that 'the jungle is neutral'. It favours the hunted rather than the hunter; it is with the former that the initiative lies since he always has the choice of when and where to attack, and there is always the jungle behind him into which he can retreat. To search the jungle for an enemy is like walking into a great waterfall and hoping that you will be neither crushed nor drowned.

In the early part of 1951 I flew out to Malaya to join the 1st Battalion of the Queen's Own Royal West Kent Regiment, stationed at Kuala Kubu Bharu, some thirty miles north of Kuala Lumpur. The Battalion had preceded me by sea—I had been appointed Adjutant and followed later with a small rear party.

In spite of the heat and the humidity, Malaya must surely be one of the most colourful and exciting countries in the world. As I left the aircraft the heat from the ground came up and hit me like a blast from an open oven. There was snow on the ground when I left England and within three days I, with my very white knees, faced a temperature in three figures.

One of the first things I had to do after my arrival at the Battalion was to get to know the new Padre. I did not appreciate it at the time, but the man I was to meet was to become a legend. The Reverend George Bedford was not blessed with a military figure by any stretch of the imagination. I first saw him walking across the parade ground. He moved with a slight stoop and his arms swung at his sides as though they were attached to his shoulders by strings over which he had no control. He was wearing khaki drill shorts and tunic, unlike the rest of the Battalion who were dressed in 'jungle green' light battle-dress. It looked, from where I stood, as though he had just emerged from a downpour of rain and his khaki drill resembled wet brown paper.

I shouted to him, 'Padre! What are you doing walking across the square? Don't you know that you walk round the square and not across it? You walk round the square like you walk round a font!'

The Reverend George Bedford stopped dead in his tracks and saluted; at what, or to whom he was saluting he had not the vaguest idea. He slowly looked round and saw me standing at the door of my office, and with what can only be described as a saunter, he came towards me. This man had a round, cheerful face and large grey eyes which twinkled behind ill-fitting spectacles.

'Sorry about the short cut across the square, sir, I will have to give more study to these military mysteries. What do you know about fonts, anyway?' He stood smiling at me as he would to a choirboy who had got chocolate on his surplice.

'I know a damned sight more about fonts, apparently, than you do about military mysteries, Padre,' I replied. 'What on earth are you dressed in khaki for? Are you being posted to the Middle East?'

He gave me a very old-fashioned look and said, 'Well, you see, I was posted to the Middle East, but the powers that be changed their minds at the last moment. Another of those military mysteries!'

I have never changed my view about padres and doctors; they are either superlative, or pretty useless. I had a feeling that this padre was going to cause me trouble, and I was right.

It was not very long after this first meeting with George Bedford that I was to learn just how skilful he was at getting his own way. He came to my office one morning looking much smarter than usual. After saluting like a jumping jack, he asked if I would publish in Part I Orders that there would be a compulsory church parade on the following Sunday. I laughed and told him that such an order would contravene Queen's Regulations; there was no longer any such thing as a 'compulsory' church parade—those days had gone for ever. He then said, 'I'll have to see the Colonel then.'

'But do,' I replied, 'he will give you the same answer that I have given you.'

That evening the Colonel spoke to me. He said, 'The Padre came to see me this afternoon. He has made a wonderful job of building the new church. He showed me around. Marvellous what he has done with grass and bamboo. He wants to test the acoustics, and I have agreed that the men can be marched to church after your Sunday morning parade for this purpose. It's not a church parade—it's just for the acoustics.' I was speechless. I did not know then that he had persuaded the Bandmaster to provide the music—for the purpose of testing the acoustics!

On the following Sunday morning at the end of the usual drill parade the men were duly marched by the band and drums to the church. There was much groaning and moaning and I could already hear the question being asked in the House, 'Why are troops in Malaya having compulsory church parades contrary to Queen's Regulations?'

The men took their places in the pews. George announced the first hymn. The reaction of the congregation was not difficult to forecast—the men sang with great gusto. So loud were their voices, and not altogether in tune, that I thought any terrorists within miles would think that we had gone mad.

Following a raucous 'Amen', the Reverend George Bedford said he would just say a few words—to test the acoustics for future sermons. He moved down to the front pews. 'Now I want to tell you about one of the oldest men in the Old Testament. He was lecherous, cruel and pernicious—and he had many women in his life.' At this astounding revelation there was not a man who did not prick up his ears—this test, if it continued in this way, was going to be a test worth listening to! But it did not continue in this vein. George Bedford gave everyone present a roasting on their conduct in general and their behaviour in the canteen on the previous evening in particular. When he had finished with his admonition he said, 'Come back next Sunday and I will tell you about the lecherous life of that man in the Old Testament.'

Needless to say, on the following Sunday the church was full, and on every Sunday after that. He never did tell us about the lecherous life of that man in the Old Testament!

George became, and still remains, the best friend I have had. This I believe can also be claimed by many soldiers with whom he served. There was the time when three soldiers lay dead in the jungle and because they were of different religious denominations no one appeared to want to take the responsibility of trekking through the *ulu* in order to give them a proper burial. George Bedford heard about it, and without orders and without knowing who the men were, he arranged for some volunteers to accompany him to the bodies. Those three soldiers had a decent burial. The story of this man's service to man could fill this book; he had the gift of the gods—and I hope he will forgive me for putting it like that. He was invariably referred to by the troops as 'George the God-Botherer'.

In the early stages of 'the emergency' the advantage was with the C.T.s, and it was not until later that security forces gained the initiative by taking a number of co-ordinated steps. The civilian

**Der Reichsführer-‡‡**
RF/M

(1) Berlin SW 11, den *22.* Januar 1945
Prinz-Albrecht-Straße 8
Feld-Kommandostelle.

Mein lieber Krafft!

Recht herzlichen Dank für Ihren
Brief vom 10.1. und die ausgezeichnete
Arbeit über den guten Einsatz des ‡-Pz.
Gren.Ausb.u.Ers.,Btl.16 in den Kämpfen
um Arnheim.

Ihnen und Ihrem Regiment meine
herzlichen Wünsche,

Heil Hitler!

Ihr

*H. Himmler.*

The letter that Reichsführer Himmler sent to Major Krafft after the battle of
Arnhem congratulating him on his part in the defeat of the British 1st Airborne
Division. The letter is dated 22 January 1945.

Gordon Horner, that great war artist, captured the scene as the Americans arrived at Oflag 79. The German guards gave up without any resistance. However, there were many prisoners in the camp who were not fit enough to give their liberators a welcome, and some were so ill that they could not believe they were free men again after four years in captivity.

(*Opposite page*) Corporal Tom Wilson: a photograph taken early in the war. He is wearing the badge of the Royal Corps of Signals. (*Below*) Corporal Tom Wilson— after the battle of Arnhem. His parachute badge is on his right arm. His face, bearing the marks of war, is in striking contrast with the earlier photograph. It is now the face of a great soldier.

(*Left*) The blowing-up of the King David Hotel in Jerusalem on 22 July 1946. Both Arabs and Jews committed themselves to violence, the British Army fair game for both.
(*Right*) A burnt-out army vehicle in a Tel Aviv street after yet another violent riot.

(*Left*) Jeep convoy heading south through the desert of Jordan. I am standing up in the last vehicle.
(*Right*) Ghengis Khan: of all the dogs I have loved he was the greatest. He is wearing the special boot made to protect his injured front paw.

H.R.H. Princess Marina, Duchess of Kent, inspecting the 1st Battalion, The Queen's Own Royal West Kent Regiment, before their embarkation for Malaya in 1951. I am on H.R.H.'s right and behind her is Major-General W. P. Oliver, C.B., O.B.E., Colonel of the Regiment.

(*Above left*) Johnny Pannell, D.C.M. He was the only soldier who made me feel that I was being commanded and at the same time that he was only doing his duty and protecting me. If Johnny was not the original 'rogue soldier' he was a magnificent successor—these two words sum up the qualifications of a good batman. Johnny was Irish and a treasure.

(*Above right*) Tom Masters; bachelor, rubber planter, survivor of a Japanese prison camp, the soldier's dream of a 'pukka sahib', an English gentleman and one of the most modestly courageous men I have known outside the Services.

(*Below left*) Two very dead communist terrorists brought back from the jungle for identification purposes—an unpleasant task for young National Servicemen. The severed head had been blown off during the action and it was brought back to prove that there had been three 'kills' and not two.

(*Below right*) Men of 'B' Company towing me out of Rawang camp in my jeep. The board fixed to the radiator had the words 'You know me feller' painted on it.

Northern Command Cricket XI played against The Hague Cricket Club at Strensall Park, York, in July 1956. It was a splendid chance to renew old ties with Arnhem as well as to get away from a staff desk. I am telling the visitors that as I have won the toss there can be no doubt that the Dutchmen will lose the match. The team from The Hague won by 14 runs!

The corner house at Westow, fifteen miles from York, where our daily help, Mrs Duck, advised us to provide sherry for the local Meet, thereby producing dinner invitations for us for many months to come.

With the then President of Rotary International, James F. Conway, at Lake Placid in 1969. He was one of the seventeen Presidents I was privileged to serve. These men were chosen annually by the Rotary Movement from countries all over the world— on this side of the Iron Curtain. Representatives from 148 countries meet once a year to foster international understanding.

population was given protection by confining them to areas guarded by armed Malayan Police. Their residential areas were surrounded by high wire which not only kept them in during hours of curfew, but also made it more difficult for the C.T.s to penetrate these areas during the hours of darkness.

Security and intelligence activities were reorganized and intensified, with the result that information concerning the movement and activities of the terrorists and their units was carefully recorded and acted upon. With the extra security given to the civilian population and the strict enforcement of curfews, information increased. Troops lived in the jungle for longer periods and increased the number of their own ambushes to such an extent that it became far more risky for the C.T.s to leave the protection of the jungle and come out into the open to contact those working in the rubber and palm oil estates. In consequence Communist funds diminished, the civilian population became less afraid, and gradually the police and the military gained authority and respect. Above all, Field Marshal Sir Gerald Templer, G.C.B., G.C.M.G., K.B.E., D.S.O., late Chief of the Imperial General Staff—arrived on the scene. He was then General and High Commissioner and Director of Operations, Federation of Malaya, and it was from the moment he took command that inertia ceased and the feeling that there could be no end to the emergency evaporated. If the emergency in Malaya was not to drag on, a great deal had to be done. Gerald Templer not only ensured that everyone became aware of what had to be done, he took positive steps to ensure that they did it. He was not what I would describe as a lovable character; he was ruthless, but he gained the immediate respect of everyone because his policy produced results and not excuses. It was his policy and personal command which was the greatest single factor in bringing the emergency to an end. He was a great professional.

Malaya was not just another area of the world which had an insurgent problem, it was an 'emergency' of the foulest kind. I once visited a planter's rubber estate, Lima Blas, near Trolak, only a few minutes after an 'incident'. A pregnant woman had been disembowelled while her husband was tied to a rubber tree and made to watch; he was subsequently slashed with a parang at the back of his head—his brains fell out. I am sure he was glad to die.

I mention this, one of many similar incidents, to emphasize the great provocation and yet restraint of the Malayan police and British troops who were sometimes accused of being too rough. For example, Communist Terrorists who had been killed in the jungle were sometimes brought out by troops with their unsightly bodies tied to bamboo poles. This was not because soldiers wished to carry extra weight for long distances, or because they were barbarians; it was because identification of killed bandits was necessary. Unlike the C.T.s the security forces could not just shoot at anyone. In my opinion, it was not a bad thing for the local populace to see that the bandits did not always win.

The British regiments serving in Malaya in the early 1950s were comprised mainly of National Servicemen, not all of whom enjoyed their enforced enlistment or the unpleasantness of jungle fighting and separation from home. However, no praise can be too high for the spirit and endeavour of the National Servicemen who served in Malaya. They arrived from England white of skin and unaccustomed to a tropical climate and they were farther away from home than they had ever been. But I suspect that when they returned to England on completing their service there were a great number of mothers, sisters and girlfriends who hardly recognized the boy who had left home and was now returned a complete man—a man who had seen and experienced the best and the worst.

Many National Servicemen died in Malaya, and not always in combat. I remember a private soldier who was on sentry duty at the main gate of the Battalion camp at Kuala Kubu Bahru. It was late at night and there was a party in progress at the local police headquarters. A European civil engineer left the party in his car to obtain more liquid refreshment. He had to pass the main gate of our camp in order to reach his bungalow. He was challenged by the private soldier on sentry duty, and he failed to stop. The soldier fired one shot, strictly in accordance with his orders. By fearful chance that one shot went through the back of the car, through the driving seat and into the spine of the civil engineer. He died before dawn. What a dreadful tragedy! However, there was worse to come. The soldier had to face the ordeal of an inquiry by a civil court which found that the incident was 'justifiable homicide'. This very young soldier was a normal, decent serviceman, who had complied strictly with his orders, but that fact did not relieve his remorse. In view of the circumstances he was sent back to England. Tragically, he committed suicide before reaching home. He died because he did his duty—and because his duty pressed him to action—the consequences of which he found unable to bear.

The jungle in Malaya is humid and in parts so thick with undergrowth that progress is often limited to yards in the hour. It is also mountainous and the ground is sodden from torrential rain; the humidity gives off a sickly smell that is not easily forgotten. There are tigers and elephants, but I never saw either except as a skin on the floor or as a foot made into a doorstop. However, I encountered hundreds of leeches, and compulsory blood trans-fusions were frequent! After a few days in the *ulu* the skin becomes white and pappy and in consequence jungle sores, sweat rash and prickly heat are frequent companions.

I was very fortunate during my service in Malaya to have as my batman Private 'Johnny' Pannell, D.C.M., a staunch Roman Catholic. I always had the good luck to find outstanding soldiers as my batmen. It was not because I can claim any credit for selecting them, it was more often than not a question of who would volunteer for the job—Pannell volunteered! He was not a tall man, five feet five inches, slight of build, wiry and with a very large cobra tattooed on his back. When he flexed his muscles the cobra was made to sway from side to side. He had seen service in India and had held every rank up to sergeant several times, each time being demoted for some misdemeanour, and subsequently pro-moted again for his excellent qualities. 'Johnny' was an outstanding batman—and many more things besides.

Soon it became the custom each evening for Johnny to fetch me a tot of whisky from the officers' mess and bring it to my *basha*; at the same time he would bring two bottles of iced beer for himself, carrying one bottle in each pocket. He would proceed to pour the beer into my silver tankard, after having given me a whisky, and would then propose a toast. It was always the same: 'My very best respects, sir. I have charged the refreshment to *our* mess bill. Good luck to us both!'

Johnny was not the kind of soldier with whom it was wise to challenge a personal ritual. I tried it only once, and felt rather taken aback when he suggested to me that in battle areas officers and their batmen shared everything! After that, I dared question the ritual no more, indeed, I came to enjoy it. George Bedford often took a sundowner with me and he once inquired if it was my mess bill or his that had been debited. Johnny answered, pointing a finger upwards, 'You only share your mess bill with Him, sir!'

With possibly one exception, I believe that Pannell feared neither man nor beast. The exception came to my notice at Shorncliffe, in Kent, before we left for Malaya. The guard commander of the camp reported to me early one morning that my batman was in the guard-room locked in a cell. I asked what offence he had committed and was told that he had not committed any offence, but had volunteered to be put under close arrest. I ordered the guard commander to release him at once and to bring him to me. When Pannell came to my office I asked him what he thought he was doing putting himself under arrest. He explained that his mother-in-law had suddenly arrived to stay the night with his family in their quarter. He had gone out and got drunk and decided he would rather spend the night in the guard-room than face his mother-in-law!

It was while I was away from the Battalion in Singapore, meeting my wife and daughter who had travelled out from England by sea seven months after my arrival, that Johnny got into trouble. This time it was with the R.S.M.! Johnny was an 'old soldier' and would stand no nonsense from 'char-wallahs' and in consequence a fight ensued following a disagreement about a purchase. Had the char-wallah not been an Indian it would have been obvious that he had received a black eye. The R.S.M. heard of the fight and in my absence, and knowing Pannell's history, he ordered him to undertake escort duties as a punishment.

Escort duties comprised meeting troops returning from jungle patrols in transport, soft-topped 3-ton trucks, which would leave the camp and rendezvous with the returning patrol at a pre-arranged point on a road near to the jungle edge, often in one of the rubber estates. These vehicles needed an armed escort on their way out to meet the returning patrol, usually comprising two or three men to each vehicle. It was for these duties that Johnny was ordered by the R.S.M. and it was on Ulu Caledonia Estate, on 22 October 1951, having picked up a returning patrol, that Johnny Pannell had his finest hour.

The vehicles, full of tired troops, were unable to travel very fast down the winding and narrow road. As they made their way back to camp through the rubber estate of Ulu Caledonia they were ambushed by some forty Communist terrorists. The ambushers were hidden from view on the high banks. Without any warning a hail of bullets rained into the small convoy. There was no cover, and the leading vehicle came to a halt and blocked the road—the driver was killed by the first burst of fire.

The officer in command, Captain Eric Deed, was riding in the front truck next to the driver, and he also was killed instantly. Eric was the son of a retired ironmonger from Margate in Kent. He was the finest poker player that I ever faced and one of the most amusing. He always carried a pocket chess set with him and would often set up a game and play against himself while in an ambush position. He was the kind of man who had the rare mixture of great gentleness and enormous guts. The only other officer in the party, 2nd Lieut. Gregson, was seriously wounded in the chest.

The situation was almost impossible since the patrol was trapped and the terrorists were able to shoot at will. As the troops jumped out of the vehicles they were exposed to fire from all sides. The only cover was underneath the vehicles and therefore it was difficult to return the fire of the terrorists.

The object of the ambush was to capture arms. The C.T.s approached in ones and twos, but failed to overrun the position. Unable to subdue the survivors of this gallant patrol, they rolled grenades down the slopes from the high ground.

Eventually, Johnny Pannell found that he was the only survivor who could take command. The official record states that 'By moving about with complete disregard for his own safety, he inspired those left who could fight to beat back rush after rush. Finally, after about an hour, the terrorists withdrew. Pannell had been hit four times, but in spite of these wounds he managed to reach the bungalow of the local planter in order to telephone B.H.Q. and ask for help.'

When help arrived the signs of the desperately fought engagement were clear for all to see. A 3-ton lorry, a scout car and a 15-cwt truck were spaced out over to some 100 yards on the estate road. All tyres were punctured and the windscreens of the vehicles were smashed; the unarmoured vehicles were riddled with bullet holes and the Bren gun mounting was shattered. In the leading truck, in the positions from which they had been firing, were one officer, ten other ranks and three Iban trackers, all dead. There was not one single unwounded soldier left. The bandits had also suffered casualties and their dead were strewn across the carnage.

For this action, Johnny Pannell gained headlines in the local press and was granted an immediate award of the D.C.M.

I read about this action in a newspaper while I was on leave in Singapore, and I returned with all haste to Kuala Lumpur to visit Johnny in hospital. His first words to me were, 'I'm sorry about all this, sir. The fact is that while you have been away I have bashed the char-wallah and one or two bandits.'

He was concerned that I had returned from leave just to visit him in hospital and he was worried that there was no one back at camp who could look after my kit. He talked quickly and in short breaths. Were the family OK? Did they enjoy the prospect of living in Malaya? He was sorry, but our mess bill was rather high this month. It was typical of him to stress the unimportant and omit the important. Not a word about his wounds, the battle he had just fought, or come to that, the reason why the R.S.M. had put him on escort duties!

As we left Johnny in Kinrara Hospital he said, 'The R.S.M. said I was unreliable. That's not true, is it, sir?' Through his outward toughness a little hurt could penetrate very easily—that one word 'unreliable' had hurt him deeply. As I shook his hand, with a wink I said, 'If you are not back on duty in about two days I won't have anyone to drink my health each night, so you'd better get a move on!' However, he never did come back to duty in Malaya and as a result the size of my mess bill decreased.

Johnny was sent back to England; his wounds had been serious. He was posted to the Regimental Depot, Maidstone, where he was once again promoted to corporal, but soon afterwards he had to accept his discharge on medical grounds. The Army had been Johnny's life and the pension which he was awarded was a pittance and nothing like enough to support him and his family who lived in a 'prefab' in Battersea. He and his wife had to find jobs to make ends meet. Johnny accepted a job which he was really not fit enough to do. He was a proud one!

Years later I visited him and his family, just before Christmas. He introduced me to his five sons who were lined up in single file as though on guard inspection. They all stood to attention and answered, 'Yes, sir!' to every question almost before I had asked it. This was 'Johnny's Regiment', and he was, justifiably, very proud of them. In a strange way I felt his pride—they were chips off the old block.

I had brought a few small presents with me, but for the youngest son I had brought my electric Hornby train set which I had treasured since my youth. Johnny, as well as his young son, was thrilled and explained that he could not offer me a present—things were a bit tight. Then with a sudden cry of delight he said, 'I know what I can give you, sir!' He went to a drawer and brought out a box which I instantly recognized. 'Please take this, sir, I really would like you to have it.' It was his Distinguished Conduct Medal! I declined, but I believe he was satisfied because I told him that I would never have a greater compliment paid to me, no matter how long I lived. Johnny knew that I meant it.

The commercial importance of Malaya was not derived only from its geographical position, but also from its natural resources, rubber and tin being by far the most important. To a lesser extent rice, pineapples, copra, coconut and palm oils were also produced. In 1949 the population was about 2,000,000, of whom 22,000 were Europeans and Australians. Because Malaya was the largest tin-producing country in the world and synthetic rubber had not replaced natural rubber it was an area of great commercial interests. Most of the tin mines and rubber estates were managed by Europeans, many of whom had lived in the country for a very long time and regarded it as though it were their own.

The men of this 'white' contingent of the multi-racial peninsula were not all cast in the same mould, but they had one quality in common—they were all technicolor characters, from the strong to the apathetic. The emergency demanded great courage from them, especially those who had wives, since they had to continue to produce the tin and the oil under conditions of extreme danger. They were very much exposed and labour problems caused by the intimidation of the Communist terrorists did not help. Life for the 'white' civilian who lived outside the main towns was no sinecure in early 1950; many had lived in the country before the war and had experienced Japanese hospitality during the occupation. The activities of the Communist terrorist brought back unpleasant memories of not so long ago.

During the emergency many Europeans lost their lives for no other reason than that they were carrying out their normal duties. I spent many nights under the roofs of planters' bungalows, and I never had a good night's sleep on these occasions. Most bungalows were guarded by Malay police (Mata Mata) who were trustworthy, loyal and enthusiastic, but even these qualities did not reassure me. I always kept a loaded revolver under my pillow and one ear awake.

The opportunity to come to know a number of planters came when I assumed command of 'B' Company. Just how and why I was given that command is explained later. Tom Masters lived on Lima Blas estate in Perak, north of Tanjong Malim. His bungalow was situated at the top of a *bukit* (small mountain) and to approach it one had to cross a rickety bridge and drive along a track which wound its way in steep spiral to the summit. As one climbed higher and the sharp bends in the road became sharper the air became noticeably cooler. At last you came to a halt in front of the bungalow, the whole of which was surrounded by jungle orchids, frangipani, bougainvillea and waving palms. To the east were the mountains and in all other directions as far as one could see were the rubber and palm oil trees comprising Lima Blas. The beauty of the place was breathtaking.

Tom ran his estate and his household with the precision of a military machine, and the whole place had the mark of efficiency which is only achieved by those who are completely dedicated to their work. His labourers were happy and his personal servants devoted to him. In this atmosphere it was difficult to imagine the situation which inspired Somerset Maugham to write his story, 'The Letter', even though the events on which his story was based occurred only a few miles away.

Curry tiffin at Lima Blas was an adventure in addition to being the best curry in the state of Perak; indeed, it was known from Perlis to Johore. Troops never passed through the estate without Tom's knowing of their presence and few passed without receiving at least one glass of cold beer. There was never any trouble in obtaining volunteers for a patrol on Lima Blas estate! The men called Tom Masters 'Sahib Gunga Lima'. I think he reminded them of a gentleman of another age about whom they had read, or thought they had read. Sandy hair, bristling moustache, straight back, and slightly bloodshot eyes which seemed to burn through you.

He tolerated fools not at all. He was a bachelor—women made

him nervous, so he said. He had been a prisoner-of-war and served in Changi Jail and in coalmines in Japan. Although he lost everything during the war and had to start all over again, I never heard him speak bitterly. He survived, he thought, because he had been hardened by pre-war whisky! Our friendship became close, and has continued, although Tom is now retired and spends most of his time in the Far East.

Now, Sam Brown, of Trolak Estate, also in Perak, was a character of a very different kind. He was an open-handed fire-eater and blew his top at the slightest provocation—the troops called him 'Topper' for more reasons than one. When 'B' Company first arrived on Sam Brown's estate it could do nothing right. He gave the very firm impression that he was there for our benefit rather than the reverse. He complained that the telephone extension from his bungalow to my Company office was 'a damned nuisance'; the men made far too much noise in the canteen; the Company transport was ruining his estate roads, particularly in wet weather; the barbed wire around the camp was a hazard to his cattle—two cows! He told me on one occasion that I was only the Colonel's chief clerk who had been promoted—this was presumably inspired by the time when I was Adjutant and had had words with him over the telephone about the previous company camped on his estate.

Here was a challenge! It took almost two weeks before the men of 'B' Company broke the heart of Sam Brown—one of the softest hearts I ever knew. They invited him to a 'sing-song' party in the canteen and, much to my surprise, Sam Brown accepted. Before the end of that evening Sam had danced on a table and joined in singing 'John Brown's Body'—or a near version of the original song. He was chaired back to his bungalow and to a very anxious Mrs Brown. From that night forward the men of 'B' Company could do no wrong in the eyes of Sam Brown, and from then he was always called 'Topper', an affectionate nickname which he never lost.

Just before Christmas the Company, with much regret, had moved away from Trolak to a new area at Rawang, some fifteen miles north of Kuala Lumpur, but my family and I were invited by Sam and his wife, Hilda, to spend the Christmas break with them on Trolak Estate. We accepted and had one of the best Christmas holidays that we can remember, and in spite of the fact that the temperature was up in the nineties and that dinner was taken at 10 o'clock at night! On the return journey home we had a piece of bad luck. Our old Citroën car had front-wheel drive and took the sharp bends in the road very well at high speed. The car was overloaded with baggage and a turkey in a basket strapped to the roof did not help the balance. I drove fast because there was always the possibility of being ambushed by terrorists, particularly with a woman and small child in the car. It was a case of putting your foot down hard on the pedal until you reached your destination. We had reached the Kanching Pass and almost completed the journey when a wild pig ran out from the side of the road in front of the car. I was travelling too fast to stop or to swerve and the car hit the poor beast amidships. It was thrown into the air and over the top of us, much to the consternation of the turkey, whose gobbling reached a very high pitch. I stopped at once, and any remorse I might have had evaporated with the thought of roast wild pig for dinner that evening.

The pig was lying in the middle of the road some forty yards behind and appeared to be very dead. I got out of the car and started to run back to where it lay, but before I had covered half the distance a civilian bus drew up beside my prize. I shouted, but with no effect. Five or six Chinese jumped off, caught hold of the pig by its legs and threw it on to the luggage rack of the bus, which had already started on its way again. The whole thing happened in a flash—my pig had been purloined under my nose! My dreams of roast wild pig for dinner had vanished—and I swore in English, Malay, Tamil and Cantonese. The bus drove past me as I stood in the middle of the road fuming and all the passengers were laughing their heads off—so were my wife and young daughter. I swore, again, and from the sounds coming from the turkey on the top of the car I think he was swearing too!

My wife and daughter, now aged four, were housed in a bungalow on the outskirts of Kuala Lumpur, and I managed sometimes to get home for an evening and return to the Company that same night. It was during one of these short dashes to see them that my wife and I returned to our bungalow, having had dinner at the Golf Club, to find my Company scout car waiting for me. The driver reported that some very important information had come to hand

and my second-in-command felt that I would wish to return to the Company without delay.

I got into the scout car—not the most comfortable vehicle in which to travel after a good dinner—and returned to Rawang where the Company was camped. It was as well that I did because the information was accurate—bandits were expected to appear on the Kerling Estate early next morning for the purpose of collecting money from the tappers.

I decided to use three ambush positions on the jungle edge to the south of the estate, taking one of the positions myself with Corporal Green, a Bren gunner, and my batman, Private Searle; Johnny Pannell, it will be recalled, had returned to England.

We were in position at first light, and it was not long before the tappers came to collect the latex and to cut the rubber trees. They did not appear to be aware of our presence. Time passed without any sign of the C.T.s and no sound from the direction of the other ambush positions. I had not had much sleep and was beginning to think that we had wasted our time, as we had done so many times before. The tappers finished their work and we could see the latex dripping again from the trees into the little cups provided for that purpose.

The sun was now quite high and still no sound could be heard except for the odd squawk of a bird. The information given to us appeared to have been false, or the C.T.s had changed their minds. So I told my two companions that they could stand up and smoke if they wished. Lying in an ambush position stiffens the body and exposes it to a number of midges which eat your flesh and suck your sweat—it's a mild form of torture since you can neither move nor speak.

I could never make up my mind which I loathed more: squatting in an ambush position for hours on end, no smoking, no movement and being bitten by midges, or plodding endlessly through the dank jungle on patrol. Both were tiring and a strain on the temper. You could never be sure if you were performing ridiculous antics and suffering for no purpose, or whether in fact you were in grave danger. The temptation to let your mind wander was always present, as was the tendency to concentrate on your physical discomforts—which could never be afforded. So often, after long periods of waiting in ambush or climbing up and down hills in thick undergrowth, nothing happened. The expected was always unexpected; this is not a contradiction. The possibility of a contact was ever present but contacts were so rare in proportion to the days spent in the jungle that an engagement with terrorists always came as a shock, if not a surprise. In those moments of recovering from the initial shock all kinds of things could happen, and did. It was not unknown to shoot a member of your own group in the confusion of a sudden brush—to distinguish friend from foe in dense undergrowth is difficult—something moves—your finger is on the trigger—and you shoot! Leading scouts faced the greatest risk since they were often the first to be hit by a sentry hidden beside a track leading to a bandit camp.

We had just lit our cigarettes when to our immediate right, and only ten yards away, a C.T. in uniform came walking nonchalantly out of the jungle. I am not sure who was more taken aback—the C.T. or my small group, but he and we acted simultaneously—he turned and ran and we followed in hot pursuit, firing as we went. I was astonished at the speed this bandit could run; he ran, zig-zag, and in spite of being hit several times he kept on running. He fell, got up and ran on again until at last, with a great leap in the air, he collapsed into a ditch. No creature could have survived the shots that we put into that bandit. When we reached him at the ditch he had at least ten shots in his body. It was not until later that we heard that our bandit was a senior member of the Malayan Communist Party, Chan Ah Yok, who was the younger brother of Mok Meng, a member of the Selangor State Committee and in charge of the Communist printing press.

Chan Ah Yok was accompanied by a woman who was also hit, but she escaped into the jungle. I think we gave preference to the right target, although we learned that Mok Meng's girlfriend had been hit in her backside and had demanded of local tappers that her wounds be dressed. Women C.T.s were as vicious as their male counterparts and just as fanatical.

As Chan Ah Yok raced along the jungle track he had scattered dollar notes in his wake—there were several hundred. It was the order that money recovered in this way must be handed to the police, and in fact it was, but I would not be surprised if some of it found its way into the Company canteen for the purpose of a celebration. To celebrate a killing must appear uncivilized, but the Communist Terrorists in Malaya *were* uncivilized—they were vermin and I never felt the slightest remorse when I saw one of them tied on a bamboo pole—or dead at the bottom of a ditch.

The time came when I had to leave 'B' Company. I received a posting to the Staff at Police Headquarters, Bluff Road, Kuala Lumpur. A few officers were seconded from the army to the police force to assist the administration during the period of rapid expansion of that remarkable body of men comprising Europeans, Malays, Chinese and Indians. I welcomed a change from 'jungle-bashing', and the opportunity to work closely with so many nationalities was a chance not to be missed. A number of European police officers then serving in Malaya had also served in the Palestine police force and I enjoyed renewing some old friendships. The Mata Mata (Malayan policemen) were of a gentle race. They were not natural fighters but they responded to their task with the greatest courage.

'B' Company had become very 'special' to me. When I first took over command it was a Company in serious trouble: the administration was poor and the discipline almost non-existent. The Battalion Commander was very concerned about this company and I asked if he would give it to me. I had been anxious to leave the Adjutant's chair and wanted to get back to commanding rather than writing other people's orders. After some careful argument the Colonel agreed to let me have the Company.

I had wasted no time in publishing the fact that I would assume command of 'B' Company and that Captain John Wilson would succeed me as Adjutant. For the first three days after joining the Company I concentrated all my attention on the administration. I only spoke to the N.C.O.s and men who were concerned with Company stores, arms and ammunition. The initial atmosphere of the Company was apprehensive. Here was yet another Company Commander—the third they had had in as many months—but this time it was the Adjutant and all soldiers know that 'all adjutants are bastards'! Perhaps the constant change of commanders was largely responsible for the poor state of this unit and now another change—and 'a bastard' at that. This appeared to be all that was needed to bring the lack of morale to the depths.

One of my first major concerns related to the new second-in-command who had just been posted to the Company, a Captain Douglas Allen. My first impression of him had not been favourable

159

and I had a distinct feeling that he did not think very highly of me. He had a casual manner and a slightly supercilious air which was almost dumb insolence. I decided that the best way to deal with him was to put him under pressure without delay. I sent for him and told him that I was not satisfied with the Company accounts; I had only had an opportunity to give them a cursory glance but that had been enough to convince me that they had been badly kept. Would he give them his immediate attention and advise me as soon as he had a report to make?

On the very next morning he reported to me at Company Office. He was neatly dressed but his salute on entering was rather like what one would expect from a well-trained seal.

'Well, what do you want?' I asked.

'I've come to report on the Company accounts,' he replied.

'I don't want a report until you have completed the job,' was my rather sharp retort.

'But I have completed the job,' he said, adding, almost as an afterthought, 'sir.'

I asked him to let me see them and followed him into the outer office where the books were laid out in very neat order on a table. He told me that the cash balances were correct, the accounts were now in good order, but it had been necessary to rewrite the Company account. He had stayed up all night to complete his task, and this was the first indication I had that Doug Allen was bloody-minded. He had done a first-class job and I told him so, but I added that I was not too impressed by new brooms which swept too clean—the bristles often fell out! He did not even smile.

A few days later I gave Doug Allen an almost impossible task. He was to meet us at a point in the jungle which I could only show him on the map. Maps of the *ulu* in Malaya were notoriously difficult to read and the rendezvous which I had chosen was just about the most difficult that I could find. I was to take a patrol out for three days and on our return he was to meet us at the arranged point with rations and mail.

On the third day of that patrol we arrived at the appointed rendezvous. There was no sign of Doug Allen or his small party carrying our rations and mail. We sat and waited for nearly thirty minutes and I was just about to give the order to move off again, when out of the undergrowth stepped Doug Allen and his small party.

'Where the hell have you been?' I inquired.

'Sitting over there watching you, sir. I did not want to appear before the appointed time in case you had some special plan arranged.'

The rations were not only to hand, tea had been 'brewed-up' and the mail sorted. As I sat down to consume an excellent stew from my mess tin, Doug Allen passed me a very large whisky—in a glass, and with ice! 'I took the liberty of putting this on your mess bill, sir,' he said. 'I have brought a small ice-box with me—the men have each got a pint of iced beer.'

It took Doug and me a little time to swallow our pride. We became very close friends and remain so to this day. He proved to be the very best second-in-command that I ever had, unflappable, loyal and a perfectionist.

He only let me down once. As we waved good-bye to him as he drew out of Kuala Lumpur railway station to go home on leave, at the last moment he threw a large envelope on to the platform. Leaning out of the carriage window he called out, 'Sell my car for me, Dicky, there's a good chap. The bumph is all in that envelope. Cheerio!' With that he was gone and I was left with an old MG (TC) on my hands. It proved to be a very difficult car to sell and cost almost as much in drinks to a young planter as the price which I received. Today it would cost a fortune—I wish I had kept it for myself!

During the first two days after taking over command of 'B' Company I had the feeling that the men were waiting for me to use the 'heavy hammer'. However, by the third day I had made no move to speak to the Company and I believe that the men had reached the conclusion that I had been in the Adjutant's chair for so long that I had forgotten what real soldiering was all about. It was at this point that I decided to surprise them.

At 3 o'clock in the morning on the fourth day of my command I roused the Company Sergeant-Major and told him to get the Company on parade in the canteen in twenty minutes' time. To say that the Sergeant-Major was surprised would be an understatement, but his reaction was nothing like as great as that of the men who were dragged from their beds in the middle of the night for no other purpose than to receive a pep talk from me.

When the whole Company was assembled, I dismissed the

officers and all N.C.O.s, saying that I would speak to them later, which I did. I then told the men present what I thought of them and gave them an opportunity to say what they thought of me. I was satisfied after just fifteen minutes that we all knew where we stood.

The following morning, Company Sergeant-Major R. E. Armstrong, asked me for a private interview and requested that he be given a posting to another company. I told him that he would only get it if I found him unfit to hold his rank in 'B' Company.

It was a very tricky beginning, but I kept my word and every officer, N.C.O. and man in the Company did the same. When I left for my Staff Appointment at Police Headquarters I was towed away by the Corps of Drums following a presentation.

As I was towed out of the camp gate men on each side of the track sprang up from hiding-places and displayed boards on which had been printed sayings which I frequently used:

'It will all be over by noon!'
'You know me fellers!'
'One more trick like that, and I'll write to your mum!'
'You look like a lot of dried green pea pods!'
'Shut the bar half an hour ago. I'll give you two minutes to make up that time!'
'Zip! Zap! That one came from way back!'
'Sit down those who have not sat on a loo for two days.' After which I gave the order, 'Those sitting down stand up—go and sit on the loo and try!'

Such sayings produced laughter no matter how often repeated. Eventually, when I started one of these sayings, the men would finish it for me in loud chorus. Morale is the greatest single factor at any time—no matter by what measure it is achieved.

I still have the letter written to me by Sergeant-Major Armstrong after I had left the Company. He turned out to be the most loyal of warrant officers, and it gave me the greatest personal satisfaction to read in his letter:

'After several attempts at writing my promised letter to you, and realizing that I had made them too much like the Q.O.G. [Queen's Own Gazette] notes, I have now decided to be a little less formal.

'The farewell—but not goodbye—has left me with a sense of personal loss. Perhaps best explained by saying that I not only look up to you as my Commanding Officer, but as my friend.

'It would be superfluous for me to explain the feelings of us all when you made your final address prior to leaving your camp. Actions speak louder than words, so our subsequent actions told only too well their own story.

'How strange it seems that a little over a year ago, I could not have considered you even as a casual acquaintance, and yet now, having had the privilege of sharing camp life with you, I now rate you tops, and thank providence for having known you.

'Believe me sir, I am going to miss you like Hell, but fortunately I shall never forget your power of command and your many achievements and sayings that endeared you to all of us. Thus then do I salvage a little of your influence to make it worth the while to carry on.

'With a Bam, Barff and a Jiggery Pop, a familiar figure, complete with smile, has just arrived at the Sergeants' Mess. The members hurry to the bar to partake of a bottle, plus the usual leg-pulling before the dart is thrown with unerring aim into the bull—"Well a guy can dream—can't he?" '

I have no doubt that the British soldier will always respond favourably to leadership. As an individual perhaps he would not claim to be an intellectual, but one hundred soldiers together seem to acquire a collective wisdom. I often think that annual reports on officers would be very illuminating if written by the men they command. The reports might not be of grammatical excellence, but they would be accurate—and sometimes penetratingly so! I have found that the nicknames given to officers by other ranks invariably describe them with great accuracy.

Through my Staff duties at Federal Police Headquarters I had the good fortune to get to know Too Joon Hing who was a 'volunteer' senior police officer stationed at Ipoh. On one of Too Joon's visits to Kuala Lumpur he invited me to join him for dinner at the Chinese Club, often called 'The Millionaires' Club', for the obvious reason. I accepted the invitation with enthusiasm because I had heard that the standard of hospitality was of a very high order and something not to be missed.

On arrival at the club I found myself sitting at a round table with some dozen other people. We were all drinking 'stingers' (whisky with a lot of iced-cold soda water). Opposite me sat a very handsome young Malay. He was beautifully dressed and I could hear that he spoke English fluently. My host asked me if I would go around the table and sit next to this young man. He would like me to talk to him about the Army since he was shortly to join the Federation Regiment. My seat was comfortable so I saw no reason why this young man should not come and sit next to me, but Too Joon pressed me to move and as his guest I could do nothing but accede to his wish. I got out of my chair and moved to one next to this young man who told me that in a few days' time he would also be a commissioned officer in the Army. He explained that he had had very little experience but was looking forward to joining his Regiment. After questioning him and forming the opinion that his military training had been very slight, I ventured to suggest that it was unlikely that he would be granted a commission in so short a time without further training and more experience. Would it be fair to the men he would command? I was rather outspoken in my views. He said that all plans had been made, so I changed the subject. I was much impressed by his knowledge of general affairs and his confident courtesy, but I failed to understand how he imagined, in spite of his academic qualifications, that he was going to receive an *immediate* commission.

On the way into dinner I asked Too Joon who was this charming young Malay to whom he had insisted that I spoke and he replied, 'Oh, he is the son of the Sultan of Selangor.'

I did not enjoy my Chinese chop very much that evening, since I was more than conscious that I had put my head into the tiger's mouth and in consequence would probably be sailing for England sooner than I had planned. I envisaged being summoned by the Chief Commissioner of Police to report to his office and to be prepared to explain why I considered that the son of the Sultan was not yet ready or qualified to take a commission in the Federation Regiment. My whole evening was ruined.

I need not have feared since nothing happened until three days after the dinner party; on this day I received an invitation to take 'refreshments' at the Sultan's residence. It was a memorable experience and confirmed to me that Malays surely have the most gracious manners in the world.

The three years which I spent in Malaya were just about enough.

Although it is a country of great beauty the climate eventually saps your energy and you long to wear clothes that do not require to be changed three times a day. There is very little to choose between living in excessive heat or in the bitter cold, but if I had to choose it would be the cold. It is easier to get warm when you are cold than to get cool when you are very hot. It is said that those born in Britain are able to acclimatize themselves anywhere in the world, be it hot or cold, but I never became used to Malaya.

We sailed out of Singapore harbour with mixed feelings, particularly about the future. However, we left with a great host of memories. There was the planter who kept his gin in lemonade bottles in his refrigerator as a means of disguise in order that his wife could not check on his consumption. There was the planter who collected butterflies and moths—this hobby cost him his life—he was killed by bandits while chasing a butterfly. Our Chinese servants had become part of the family and we would miss them, and we certainly would no longer be able to afford a cook, a housekeeper, a nanny and a gardener on our return to England. There was the final party at which we had said goodbye to all our friends; in order to finance this party and clear an overdraft at the Hong Kong and Shanghai Bank I had to sell two Persian carpets—at a loss!

A thousand memories slipped over the horizon with the tops of the palm trees, of which one of the most outstanding was the visit paid to the Regiment by H.R.H. Princess Marina, the late Duchess of Kent, Colonel-in-Chief. The risk to her personal safety was very great, but at no time did she lose her calm poise or show concern—she was just determined to see *her* Regiment while she was in the Far East and nothing, not even bandits, would stop her!

Our return to England would produce problems. I did not know where I would next be posted; there would be no military accommodation available for us and my daughter would have to be found a school to attend. These are routine matters which every Serviceman has to face regularly if he is not to be separated from his family.

*'Until time shall bring all of us home'*
Last line of School Song

# 7

# *Epilogue:*
# *The Beginning of the End*

By 1954 I was thirty-five years of age and had an urge, before it was too late, to serve again with a parachute battalion. I reported to the Airborne Depot at Bulford. The barracks had not changed very much since I had last seen them in 1942, except that I think they were even smarter since there was now more time for 'bull'. Colonel Geoffrey Pine-Coffin was in command; it was good to see him again and on my first night in Mess we talked into the early hours about 'the old days'.

Those returning to the Regiment were required to take the parachute course and qualify for a second time. There was no question of favours for past service or automatic acceptance, and rightly. I joined a training squad without badges of rank—rank was ignored while undergoing the course since an officer had to be at least as fit as the men he commanded. Of course, the other ranks knew who the officers were and took advantage of the circumstances to pull their legs. On one occasion when I failed to clear the vaulting horse a member of my squad called out, 'Is that how you did it during the war, sir? You must have terrified everybody!'

Neither the physical standard nor the high morale had declined. After two attempts, I failed to pass the course, in spite of every assistance given to me. The wound in my leg split open and I had to face the fact that I was no longer fit for parachuting. This was hard to accept, but worse was to follow. A medical board downgraded me to 'base everywhere—permanent'. This medical grading meant that I was doomed to serve on the Staff, or be posted to extra-regimental employment, for the rest of my service.

The realization that I would never serve again with soldiers had a profound effect on me. I felt as though I was a spent force, as indeed I was. I would never again look up through the rigging lines to a silken canopy or hear the wind whispering through the shrouds.

To serve on the staff in peacetime is often frustrating, particularly if you are not interested in the branch to which you are posted. It means that you are confined to a desk all day and surrounded by piles of paper and files upon which you make recommendations which are often overruled or ignored. Extra-regimental employment can be even worse; these appointments can range from administering a transit camp to being a permanent president of courts martial; with no thought of disrespect to these appointments, they were not my *métier*. The Services cannot operate without good staff officers, but I was not a good staff officer, which no doubt accounts for my jaundiced opinion.

I was posted to Headquarters, Northern Command, at York, where I remained chairborne for three years. Strangely enough I enjoyed this appointment. I captained the Command cricket team for a little while until my leg let me down again. I experienced Yorkshire wit and grit and the marvellous hospitality for which that county is famous. I rented a house at Westow, a small village about seventeen miles north-east of York. The house was one of those large granite affairs which are as difficult to keep clean as they are to keep warm.

On the second day after we had moved in I was having my breakfast when there came a rasping knock on the back door. I found that my caller was a middle-aged lady, small in stature and with an expression on her face that left me in no doubt that she had called on business and was in a hurry to get it settled. She spoke very quickly and with a broad Yorkshire brogue. I couldn't understand a word she said, so I called for my wife to interpret. The lady's name was Mrs Duck and she wanted to become our daily help. When I heard this I roared with laughter which, of course, was misunderstood by our caller because she did not know that our previous daily helps had been called Mrs Parrott, Mrs Body and Mrs Dewitt, pronounced 'Dooit'.

Mrs Duck proved to be a gem. She told us that it was the custom when the local hunt met outside our house for us to provide sherry for all those present and to pass it through the large window in the drawing-room to those gathered outside. I took a very poor view of this custom but had not the courage to ignore it; so, when the hunt met sherry was duly passed through the drawing-room window! However, Mrs Duck was a wise one, since her advice led to our receiving invitations during the next twelve months to dinner parties all over the Ridings.

My final months in the army were spent with the Directorate of Manpower Planning at the War Office, now the Ministry of Defence—a rose by any other name! I hated every moment of it. I was not suited to be a civil servant, in or out of uniform, for that is what Army officers become once they are loaned to the Ministry which is a Government department. I have nothing against civil servants, indeed, I have a great sympathy for them. However, my limited experience leads me to believe that their numbers in military establishments could be drastically reduced without any great loss of efficiency.

In 1958, I applied to resign my commission. My application was refused. A year later I applied again and this time my application was granted under the 'golden bowler' scheme. The terminal grants were generous, but the pensions totally unrealistic. I am unable to accept the fact that pensions granted to ex-Servicemen do not remain constant according to age, rank and service. Those who retired in 1959 have pensions which today are only a fraction of the pensions given to Servicemen who currently retire with the same period of service, with the same rank and at the same age. It seems that all governments are unsympathetic to those who are unable to bring political or economic pressures to bear upon them. Unpleasant as this may sound, it is the truth, as any soldier or widow of a soldier will confirm. At the present time some widows receive half-pension, while others receive one-third; this is not only iniquitous but a disgrace. The soldier cannot strike and there are heavy punishments for mutiny; he has no trade union and therefore is never an industrial, or political threat through the media to any government.

It is a traumatic experience to leave the Army after a long period of service. Generally, in civilian life there is a prejudice against ex-Service personnel and the use of military rank is often regarded as an affectation. What many civilians do not appear to know is the fact that a regular commission granted by the Monarch is an honour and to fail to use military rank can be misunderstood by those who appreciate its significance. Time spent in the Services is generally considered non-productive.

When I retired I had not the faintest idea what I was going to do, or indeed what I could do. I applied for a number of appointments advertised in the daily press and in a short time I learned a great deal from the interviews I was granted. At one I faced a panel of six men, including the chairman whom I presumed had a casting vote should that prove to be necessary. The vacancy was for a security officer to a very large concern; it was at the time when Nikita Krushchev was returning from America to Moscow following talks with the President of the United States. I was asked the question, 'What do you think was in the mind of Krushchev during his flight back to Russia?'

I replied that my guess was probably wildly inaccurate, but no one except Krushchev could prove it, so what was the point of the question?

I was answered sharply with the retort, 'To test your powers of imagination'! On returning home after that interview I told my wife that there was not the slightest chance of my being given that appointment. Strangely enough, three days later it was offered to me! It is only fair to add that my arrogance was no doubt stimulated by the fact that I had already been offered another appointment.

At an earlier interview I had been asked, 'As a regular serving officer, with experience on the staff, you have been accustomed to writing formal letters with a very stiff approach, like 'Sir, I am directed to inform you, etc.' How do you think you would be able to cope with the personal and friendly letters which you would be required to write should you be granted this appointment?'

My reply was as direct as the question, 'I have written many letters to mums and dads which did not start as you suggested. I have also written letters to a large number of widows, perhaps the most difficult of letters to write. I envisage no problems.' My inquisitor was a distinguished accountant, and although it was a perfectly reasonable question, he was generous enough to say that he had asked for the 'backhanded rebuke' which I had given him. I won his vote, as he told me some years later.

During the seventeen years following my retirement from the

Army I was to experience the splendour of the peaks as well as the depths of disappointment and frustration.

In July 1959, I assumed the appointment of Assistant Secretary to Rotary International in Great Britain and Ireland. Eight years later, following the death of the Secretary, I succeeded him as the executive officer of this unincorporated association of business and professional men.

What a fascinating appointment this was to prove to be. Previously, I had always travelled eastwards, but now my duties took me as far west as New York and Honolulu, as far south as Atlanta and Mexico, and as far as north as Montreal and Quebec. However, far more interesting than further opportunities to travel were the opportunities of personal contact with business and professional men from all over the world—excluding those countries behind the 'Iron Curtain'.

From the days of Mau Mau the policy and the problems of Apartheid had concerned and interested me. Although I had personal experience of racial problems and nationalism in other parts of the world an opportunity to visit Kenya, Rhodesia and South Africa had eluded me. However, during one of my annual visits to the United States I met J. P. Duminy, who was at one time Principal and Vice-Chancellor of the University of Cape Town. He had studied at the Sorbonne in Paris and also at Oxford. I liked 'J.P.', whom I found to be a man of compassion and intellect, of moderation and concern. I got to know him well both in America and on occasions when he visited England, and was glad to call him a good friend.

One day I travelled with him on a train journey from London to Cornwall; he was to give an address to a conference. He asked me if I thought he would be asked any questions relating to the racial problems in South Africa. I said it was almost a certainty. Would he care for me to ask him some questions which might be put to him? It might help to pass the time while we travelled westward.

I enjoyed that train journey during which the word 'apartheid' was never mentioned. 'J.P.', as he was affectionately called, believed that the dilemma presented to South Africa by the clash between the two sincere and strong desires, namely that of the small nation of four million Whites to retain complete say over its own destiny, and that of the nine million Africans in the White areas to have an effective and acceptable say in the way in which their lives were being regulated, was a situation which called for a compromise. The compromise seemed to lie somewhere between two extremes: perpetual White domination on the one hand and Black majority rule on the other. He made the point, with a slight smile, that there were no precedents which could be taken as a guide as might have been the case if during the past one hundred years or so the population of the United States of America had included some 450 million Red Indians of an earlier age, or if Great Britain had experienced an influx of some 120 million Africans from the wilds of her former colonies in Africa.

'J.P.' could not understand the dogma of majority rule. If the reins of government were going to be placed in the hands of an ethnic majority just because it *was* indigenous, could it not be said that such an arrangement would be as blatantly racial as anything racial could be? If majority rule were to consist of citizens, of whatever race or colour, who knew what government meant and were competent enough to apply their knowledge to maintain law and order, to conserve and organize the use of the nation's resources efficiently, and to administer its domestic and international affairs to the greatest benefit of all citizens, then it would be highly desirable. Unfortunately, many of the Black population of South Africa were not far removed from their early tribal way of living, and many were still given to the wiles of witchcraft and the practice of ritual murder.

I found myself thinking that it is so easy to adopt an attitude of righteousness, particularly when self-interests are not directly involved and one's knowledge is based mainly on hearsay. 'J.P.' found it hard to reconcile the uncompromising attitude taken by western governments with regard to Rhodesia and South Africa with the lack of urgency given to the Germans in the East, or to the Jews held captive in Russia. Pious pontification and political profanity appeared to provide the ingredients for inevitable disaster. The example provided by a number of States in Africa which had received independence could only emphasize the danger of surrendering authority before the recipient is qualified and competent to receive it.

I only met the Rt. Hon. Enoch Powell on one occasion, but it was a memorable one. I had been invited to spend the weekend with the Rotary Club of London at its Annual Conference at Eastbourne towards the end of 1968. Enoch Powell was the guest of honour and principal speaker and, before the Conference, had given the press and the President of the Club advance copies of what he proposed to say about coloured immigrants. The President of the Club was concerned about some of the things contained in the speech and asked me if I would approach Enoch Powell with the object of getting him to take a little of the steam out of what he intended to say. After a long discussion in his suite at the headquarters hotel I came to the conclusion that there was no chance whatsoever of his changing a word of it. He intimated that his address was a most important one, but if I did not consider that the platform of the Rotary Club of London was important enough, or sufficiently unbiased, then he would be prepared to catch the next train back to London. There was just no answer to that ultimatum.

He delivered his address, after which he received a standing ovation. I thought it was brilliant, as did many others, but the uproar which followed through the media was predictable. His masterly summary of the nation's financial problems, which formed the second part of his address, unbelievably was not even mentioned in the press.

What a totally different image this man presented in private from that which he sometimes projects from a public platform. I found it difficult to reconcile the man with whom I had had a very enjoyable dinner with the man who had fired racial statistics at a spellbound audience only a few hours before. He was charming, completely relaxed and as interested in my own problems as he was in his own beliefs. Whatever history may say of this man it will surely record that if sometimes his timing may have been at fault, his prophecies were not always unfounded.

We have dissipated the last of 'the empires' resulting from a guilt complex and only the voices claiming that we exploited our former colonies are heard. Not a word is raised in our defence. Did we not establish rubber trees in Malaya? Tea in India? Find the minerals in South Africa and give that country prosperity? Did we not plant cocoa trees in West Africa? All these countries have benefited from our influence and to a standard that they would otherwise never have reached in the same time. We continue to placate our conscience by granting large sums in financial aid, which we cannot afford, to the Third World, and just how the money is spent we can never be sure. We allow those who wish to benefit from the welfare state sit at our table and devour the benefits to which they have not contributed, and at the same time let them complain about the service. Fellowship can go too far and conscience can confuse clear thinking. The real cause of our present racial problems is the fact that we failed to see that the Third World would one day rise and we are now trying to make up for lost time. To ensure that our own children follow in our footsteps education and instruction are provided; why then should we expect the undeveloped countries to be able to govern themselves unless they have been given time and a progressive opportunity to do so? The kindergarten has suddenly found itself in the sixth form—little wonder that most of the pupils are making an arrogant mess of their tasks.

Through the kindness of Lord Grantchester in 1968, I was able to persuade Dr Franz Joseph Strauss, then Finance Minister of the Republic of Germany, to address a Conference in Blackpool. His flight in his own aircraft to our meeting-place had been delayed and he arrived at the hotel a little after 11 p.m. I thought he would be tired and wish to retire to his suite, but not a bit of it, he wanted a good meal and a pint or two of 'good draught English beer'. I had already dined long since, but joined him at his table. We sat alone since he had dismissed his staff—I am not sure if they were hungry or not. It seemed to me to be another case of 'alles aus'! Here was presented an opportunity which was unlikely to be repeated and I was determined to make the most of it.

With a pound of steak inside him, together with a pint or so of ale, Dr Franz was in remarkably good form and no worse for a long day and a tiresome journey. I found him quite relaxed and prepared to express his views, quite forcibly, on almost any subject from the excellence of the German football team to the inadequate contribution of British Forces to N.A.T.O.

I was particularly interested to hear his views on Russian policy. He believed that, for some time, the Soviet Union had been visibly anxious to establish a kind of 'cordon sanitaire' around its sphere of influence—formerly it might have been called a 'cordon Stalinaire'. Since the war Russia had attempted to create a state of revolutionary unrest beyond the borders of her own territory, but in Europe she was satisfied with the *status quo*, at least for the time being. Meanwhile, it appeared that she was concentrating on neutralizing, or at least paralysing, those countries which bordered her orbit. The preliminary aim was to produce a condominium and a network of bilateral and multilateral safeguards binding her neighbours. Once this preliminary objective had been achieved the Kremlin would find it easier to maintain the 'Socialist' bloc in Europe, to mobilize for its eventual contest with its Chinese rival and, finally, to resume its expansionist policy in Europe from a consolidated position.

I liked Joseph Strauss—and I found it not at all difficult to forget that he was an old enemy. That dinner party took place in April 1968 and what Joseph Strauss said then could be said today with no less truth and with even more conviction. Russia has reason to be satisfied with the progress of her policy which now extends to the continent of Africa and beyond.

The word 'détente' implies a cessation of strained relations and is in itself an admission that all is not well between the parties concerned. If the 'détente' breaks down the result can only aggravate an already disagreeable situation. I have never trusted a 'détente' between two parties who have diametrically opposed concepts, because neither is likely to surrender its principle; to agree to differ only defers the day of conflict. One has to face the fact that international affairs do not follow the same rules as magnetism by which unlike poles attract.

The price of freedom has to be paid for, but it is not a fixed price, nor is a final discharge ever given on payment. Eternal vigilance is imperative to prevent the bill being presented too often and with even larger debits.

Faint hearts and John Foster Dulles acquiesced at the time of the invasion of Egypt. The Suez Canal had been stolen without consultation. France and Britain decided to attack and seize the Canal. Having made the major decision and having successfully committed their forces they made a humiliating withdrawal following American pressure. How different would the situation be today if that attack had been allowed to continue to its inevitable conclusion? The withdrawal from Egypt lost us the Suez Canal and oil immediately became more costly since it had to travel by tankers around the Cape of Good Hope. This fateful decision to abandon success lit the torch which scorched Israel and set Africa alight, and the flames were fanned to fury by the wind of change. The débâcle of Suez started the stampede for national

175

independence of the States in Africa, the results of which only history can tell; the 'black' continent has never looked blacker.

One of the most dynamic men that I met was Sir Paul Chambers, when he was Chairman of the Board of Directors of I.C.I. His tremendous sense of fun and general good humour surprised me; he still had the magic of the schoolboy to thoroughly enjoy himself regardless of the fact that he carried many great problems on his mind at that time.

Here was a great man, a very likeable man. He played bridge into the early hours of the morning and made light of mistakes made by others who were nothing like as good a player as he. I also learned that he was not averse to a tot. of the very best Scotch whisky. Sir Paul had a magnetism, a quality which drew one to him whenever he spoke or laughed, or rather chuckled; but behind this carefree exterior was a mind which gave the feeling that it was ticking as precisely as an expensive watch. I suspected that it could also explode with the suddenness of an alarum!

I remember that he had very strong views about the power of the motives of individuals. He believed that people who had rigid feelings about social issues and about the need to improve the lot of the underprivileged would listen readily to those who, it was alleged, operated a system of enterprise solely for personal gain. The comparison was sometimes made between private enterprise operated with such motives and a nationalized undertaking in which the purpose was the national or social good. He thought that such a contrast was false, in that the truth could only be displayed if the motives of the *individuals* concerned were examined. He emphasized 'individuals' because he considered that the driving force of any large organization could only be derived from the motives of the individuals of which it was comprised.

There seemed to be no argument against the point Sir Paul made, but when I asked if he thought that leadership had any influence over individual motives he said, 'Yes, it can have a great deal of influence—either good or bad, according to the kind of leadership.'

A year or two after that first meeting in April 1967 I saw Sir Paul Chambers again. We had not met in the meantime. He was the Chairman at a meeting of the Institute of Directors and on that day, as no doubt on many others, he met a great many people. When I introduced myself I was both surprised and flattered that he at once remembered me. It was not until later that it dawned on me that it was probably the standard of bridge that he had recalled so clearly rather than the individual who confronted him!

I have always had a great admiration for those who are able to remember faces as well as names—and put them together correctly. I was never very good at it, but I learnt a few tricks. If you can keep the conversation going long enough something is usually said which gives a clue as to the person's identity. If the worst comes to the worst you can always say, 'Someone was talking to me about you this morning, but they referred to you as "John". That is not your usual name, is it?' You are very unlucky if your problem is not solved by the answer you receive. If luck is not with you, then confess—and laugh—if you can!

The rhetorical can be very moving at the time, but its effect is limited. I have listened to hundreds of addresses, but there are very few that have had any lasting influence upon me.

Luther Hodges, a former Governor of North Carolina and former Secretary of Commerce in the United States, was the most direct of men; so much so that he could be misunderstood on first meeting, and consequently thereafter. He once wrote to me in the following terms: 'Dear Victor, You did a very good job internationally. I like you. Keep it that way! Sincerely, Luther.'

I shall always be grateful to Luther Hodges for many kindnesses, but in particular for going out of his way to see that I met Adlai Stevenson, then the United States Ambassador to the United Nations. Adlai Stevenson was the man they said would never become President of the United States because he was far too clever, not 'too clever by half', but so brilliant that most of what he had to say when addressing an audience went over the top of their heads. This was good American fun, but I believe that there may have been more than a grain of truth in the jest.

It was in 1965 in Atlantic City that I met Adlai Stevenson. He had a marvellous sense of humour. I remember a story that he told about a preacher in Southern Illinois who was concerned about a certain lady in his congregation. One day, on her way out of church, he stopped her, shook hands and said, 'Dear Madam, I want you to know that last night I prayed for you for three hours.'

And she said, 'Well, Reverend, you needn't have gone to all that trouble; if you had called me up, I would have come right over.'

We walked along the 'board walk', so called because the

promenade along the seafront is constructed of heavy wooden planks similar to those found on seaside piers in this country. He had a quiet voice and it was not easy to catch every word he said since the noise of the tramping feet as we walked on the 'board walk' dominated all other sounds.

Risking a sharp rebuke for talking shop I asked him what was the most vexed question which faced him at the United Nations. He frowned and deep lines appeared on his forehead. He said that the development of 'camouflaged aggression' had created a new and dangerous situation. It was an aggression which was difficult to diagnose and define—so much so that it often created just the kind of confusion the instigators desired. He explained what he meant by the technique of camouflaged aggression: the Marxist ministry of truth had perfected the exercise of converting black into white, and up into down. Totalitarianism was the new democracy, Communist intervention was always liberation and counter-intervention against it was always Western imperialism. The technique of aggressive violence was always a war of national liberation, defined as an extension of the class struggle. The resulting mayhem from this activity was always blessed as a 'just' war, as distinct from all other kinds of war which were 'unjust'. The technique fomented armed attack against anyone who was not armed, or assistance to anybody else engaged in violence against established non-Communist governments.

The premature and sudden death of this man during a visit to London produced a gap in international affairs which was not easily filled. He saw the pattern of Communism very clearly, and he believed that nothing in the future was likely to divert the Kremlin from its course, détente or no détente.

Although there was great fascination as well as pleasure in meeting and talking to international personalities—and I had the privilege of meeting many more than I have mentioned—life as the general secretary to a voluntary association of business and professional men was not all social intercourse and travel. To serve as the executive officer of a general council and its seventeen sub-committees, the membership of which changes every year, was an appointment demanding a good deal of patience, tact and hard work. To be responsible for a party of forty or fifty Rotarians travelling to the United States, with their wives, once a year was enough to break the back of the strongest camel. You were

required to be a walking and inexhaustible fount of knowledge—questions ranged from 'How high is the Empire State
Building?' to 'What is for breakfast tomorrow?'

The situation of a new president each year presented its own
special problems; it sometimes produced a complete change in the
approach to previously cherished policies, changes in administrative
procedures and, above all, the need to adapt oneself to a new
personality which could range from a bishop to the headmaster of
an approved school. All the seventeen presidents whom I had the
pleasure to serve were married men and I quickly learned that their
wives were a force with which to reckon. There were many
occasions when the seemingly impossible was achieved with their
connivance. Indeed my task would have been far more difficult had
I ever had to serve a bachelor president.

I found a great deal to admire and respect in the Rotary
Movement, but as with most voluntary organizations the greatest
weakness is in the conflict of human traits, both good and not so
good, particularly in the realms of the hierarchy. I experienced
much great personal kindness and never ceased to wonder at the
unheralded and unsung service and achievements of individual
Rotarians. From time to time the strain of dealing with differing
personalities had to be endured, but this is an occupational hazard
of all professional general secretaries who do know many of the
answers, but not all of them.

There were many opportunities to meet the leaders of other
major voluntary organizations in Britain and I came to have a
great regard for the enormous contribution they make to the
welfare of our local communities. None the less, I have not the
same confidence in some of the schemes which are launched for aid
overseas—the motives are invariably splendid but the execution is
often an abortive waste of time, material and money. I cannot
accept that the losses are inevitable. The motives of those who give
voluntary service vary from fanatical dedication to personal
pleasure and prestige, but then little in this world is perfect. It is
said that the greatest achievements for mankind have been
accomplished by sinners rather than by saints, but this is no more a
whole truth than is the unfair description that all voluntary
workers are 'do-gooders'. In my opinion, voluntary service in these
islands will remain a blessing and a necessity because it not only
provides a personal need for those who serve and and are served,

but also because it fills so many gaps left exposed by the welfare state. While governments can get people to do something for nothing they will always give such people lip-service support; but as yet they are not prepared to relieve them of tax burdens related to the service which they give.

The past forty years have been an exciting period in which to live, a time in which the British Empire has vanished and the British Commonwealth of Nations continues to struggle for survival. The freedom of India was granted with haste and political expediency rather than with wisdom and it cost thousands of lives. The bearded Archbishop of Cyprus was banished, but later sat with the Monarchy—how often we have had a change of heart when it suited our political purpose. Malta no longer has the loyalty which earned that island the unique honour of the George Cross. Gibraltar hangs perilously at the tip of the Iberian Peninsula. The Gold Coast, now known by another name, is the grave of the black as well as the white man. The barbaric practices of Mau Mau were rightly condemned, but its leader was later accepted by the head of nearly every State.

The people of the British Isles who once stood shoulder to shoulder to face the mightiest war machine the world had ever seen—and for a time stood alone—are no longer completely united—there are those who wish to split the nation into fragments—and they are not all simple devolutionists. Terrorists of the worst kind are free to go about their ghastly business, and the running sore which they have produced continues to bleed. People are stunned by the increase in violence throughout the world and by the exposure of decadence and deceit in high places. The welfare state, so noble in its conception, is commonly abused and has encouraged those who are naturally lazy to become completely idle. Governments continue to find no difficulty in spending other people's money, and not always wisely. All the great leaders seem to have been killed off and only time will tell if the great world mass can do without them.

The First World War was fought to end all wars and to produce a land fit for heroes. The Second World War was fought to end aggression and tyranny. Neither achieved its aim.

The League of Nations was a dismal failure; the United Nations was to be a new beginning, but alas, apart from the 'special agencies', it has proved to be abortive and no match for the

EPILOGUE: THE BEGINNING OF THE END

situations with which it is confronted. Perhaps the contacts, nation with nation, have helped just a little, but as yet there is no unity of purpose within the United Nations except in those matters which do not affect individual national interests. Were it not for the continued generosity of the United States, the United Nations would probably go bankrupt within a year.

The farther man advances technically and the greater becomes his genius, the less he seems able to cope with his own personal emotions. Perhaps it was the beauty of Honolulu which had an effect on me when I listened to Colonel Frank Borman as he spoke of his flight to the moon in Apollo 8 in the 1960s. Perhaps it was his modesty or the fact that he spoke of the exploit as though it was something that anyone could have undertaken. Whatever it was, his words had a profound effect on me, perhaps because they were so cogent. He said that the most significant emotion which he felt during the flight to the moon was the impact of looking back to earth—not looking at the moon, but looking back at the radiantly blue and beautiful sphere that was earth. It looked so very fragile and quite unearthly. He wondered why it was that human genius could concentrate all its endeavours to build moon-shots and beyond—and yet fail to solve the harmony of man.

Richard Spender wrote: '... little men who die that the great Truths shall live.' The 'little men' have been dying since history began. On looking back down the track I ask myself why do 'little men' have to die that the great Truths shall live?

If only, through all the changing scenes of life, we could display the same solidarity and purpose as in times of dire emergency, and the consideration for others then so common, then the gods of Olympus might envy us, but how they must laugh at our frailty when the need for solidarity seems to have slipped away.

# Index

INDEX